Discussions and Democracy

Discussions and Democracy

Motivation, Growth, and the New Social Studies Classroom

Christopher T. Dague

ROWMAN & LITTLEFIELD
Lanham • Boulder • New York • London

Published by Rowman & Littlefield
An imprint of The Rowman & Littlefield Publishing Group, Inc.
4501 Forbes Boulevard, Suite 200, Lanham, Maryland 20706
www.rowman.com

86-90 Paul Street, London EC2A 4NE

Copyright © 2024 by Christopher T. Dague

All rights reserved. No part of this book may be reproduced in any form or by any electronic or mechanical means, including information storage and retrieval systems, without written permission from the publisher, except by a reviewer who may quote passages in a review.

British Library Cataloguing in Publication Information Available

Library of Congress Cataloging-in-Publication Data

Names: Dague, Christopher T., 1981- author.
Title: Discussions and democracy : motivation, growth, and the new social studies classroom / Christopher T. Dague.
Description: Lanham, Maryland : Rowman & Littlefield Publishing Group, 2024. | Includes bibliographical references. | Summary: "Discussions and Democracy: Motivation, Growth, and the New Social Studies Classroom focuses on strategies and best practices for developing and implementing seminars and deliberations. It explores the impacts of how utilizing discussion pedagogy can promote and facilitate student motivation and engagement"—Provided by publisher.
Identifiers: LCCN 2024003462 | ISBN 9781475874440 (cloth) | ISBN 9781475874457 (paperback) | ISBN 9781475874464 (epub)
Subjects: LCSH: Social sciences—Study and teaching—United States. | Democracy and education—United States. | Motivation in education—United States.
Classification: LCC LB1584 .D25 2024 | DDC 300.71—dc23/eng/20240308
LC record available at https://lccn.loc.gov/2024003462

This book is dedicated to my parents. To my late father, Jim, I hope you can look down on me from above with pride for the work I continue to do to support the well-being of young people. While I certainly wish you were still with us, I hope you know the indelible mark you left on me and the lives of all who knew you. To my mother, Karen, your tenacity and work ethic helped to create a pathway for all the success I have been able to experience. You have one of the most caring hearts of anyone I have ever known. Thank you for always being there and for always believing in me.

SPECIAL THANKS

I need to begin by thanking Tiffanie for her love and patience throughout this entire process. I could not have gotten here without you and your unwavering support. This has been a labor of love, to say the least. Your love for me and my work assuredly served as the spark I routinely needed. Thank you for being my best friend and most steadfast supporter.

I also need to recognize the hard work and dedication of Soni "Dottie" Patton. You have read nearly every single word I have written over the past decade. Your time and effort, and my appreciation, are immeasurable. Those "dots" will always be yours.

Contents

Foreword   ix
John K. Lee

Acknowledgments   xi

Introduction   1

1   The History   6

2   The Rhetoric and the Reality   19

3   The Enlightenment   31

4   The Deliberation   43

5   The Listening   55

6   The Motivation   65

7   The Support   77

8   The Community   89

9   The Skills   100

10   The Change   111

References   117

About the Author   125

Foreword

John K. Lee

*Associate Dean for Faculty and Academic Affairs,
North Carolina State University*

In an era where the landscape of education continuously evolves, *Discussions and Democracy: Motivation, Growth, and the New Social Studies Classroom* emerges as a fresh voice of innovation and practical wisdom for educators. This book is not just a collection of theories and concepts; it is a guide, a companion for educators who are navigating the challenging yet rewarding path of supporting the development of rigorous intellectual habits among students in the field of social studies.

The essence of social studies education lies in its power to mold informed, critical, and engaged citizens. Yet, the traditional methodologies often employed in classrooms have not always aligned with these lofty goals. Too often, educators center themselves in the learning process and neglect the core responsibility we have in social studies to activate and engage students in civic life. This book addresses this disconnect head-on, advocating for a shift from teacher-centered approaches to discussion pedagogy—a method that breathes life into social studies education, making it more democratic, engaging, and relevant to students.

What sets this book apart is its commitment to bridging the gap between the rhetoric of educational ideals and the reality of classroom practice. It is a response to the urgent need for methods that not only impart knowledge but also foster critical thinking, communication skills, and civic engagement. Through its focus on discussion pedagogy, the book offers a pathway for educators to cultivate these essential skills in their students, preparing them not just for tests, but for life as active, informed participants in a democratic society.

Dr. Christopher Dague, with nearly two decades of experience in both teaching and teacher education, brings a wealth of knowledge and practical insight to this work. The book is grounded in the realities of the classroom, offering real-world examples, professional vignettes, and a style of writing that is both accessible and engaging. It is a testament to the author's deep understanding of the challenges and opportunities that exist in today's social studies classrooms.

This book is not just for K-12 educators. Its foundation in robust scholarship makes it a valuable resource for scholars, professional organizations, and teacher education programs who share a commitment to democratic education. It fills a crucial gap in social studies education, offering a fresh perspective that is both comprehensive and specific in its approach to discussion-based learning.

Through the ten chapters of this book, you will embark on a journey through the history, challenges, and potential of social studies education. From exploring the turbulent past of the subject to presenting innovative strategies for classroom discussions, the book covers a wide range of topics, each crucial to the development of a democratic classroom environment.

Discussions and Democracy: Motivation, Growth, and the New Social Studies Classroom is more than just a book; it is a call to action. It challenges educators to rethink their approach to teaching social studies, to embrace methods that foster active engagement, critical thinking, and democratic values. As we navigate the complexities of the twenty-first century, this book serves as an important guide for educators committed to preparing students for the challenges of tomorrow's democratic society.

Acknowledgments

I want to thank my family. To my brother David and his family (Neva, Anja, and Aylin), your help and support over the years have had such a positive influence on me. I am forever grateful. To my stepmother Dianne, thank you for all you did for Dad and for never leaving my side. To my sister Tiffany and her family (Lee, Jonah, Brody, and Lily), our bond, throughout it all, is something that I have never taken for granted. To my Uncle Tracy, thank you for stepping in and helping to ease the loss of Dad. I will always be appreciative of you holding to your word to remain in my life forever. I also want to thank Thom and Pam Kim as well as Zachary, Olivia, and Sydnie Lubbers.

I want to acknowledge my colleagues (past and present) and friends who have been constant supporters of me, not only on this project but throughout. Thanks go to Amanda Baker, AJ Barnes, Mary Jo Bauer, Tom and Debbie Bergamine, Dr. Jack and Mrs. Britt, Jarrod Britt, Natt Bunphithak, Jerry and Patty Burch, Dr. Prentice Chandler, Carl Combs, Jeff Dallas, Dr. Heather Davis, Scott Ellis, Denise Garison, Dr. Bradley Fay, Dr. Chris Godwin, Bill and Mary Groening, Samuel P. Guy III, Matthew Hoover, Dr. Britnie Kane, Dr. John Lee, Dr. Michael Livingston, Conrad Lopes, Dr. Evan Ortlieb, Dr. Chris Marcum, Jeff Morehead, Fluff Nusbaum, Mike O'Dell, K. Scott Pope, Judy Shelton, Blair Small, Jamie Sykes, Brian Willis, Thea Weinheimer, and Lieutenant Commander Nicole Winget.

Finally, I need to thank all the countless students and players with whom I have had the great pleasure of working over the course of my nearly twenty-year career. My time at Jack Britt High School, The Citadel, and Campbell University has shaped my love of teaching, and my unfettered belief in the power of education.

Introduction

Numerous iterations of this book have floated around in my mind in recent years, causing its vision to take on many shapes. In its current form, its overarching purpose seeks to explore and bring to light numerous issues that face teachers and students daily. It seeks to provide an avenue for hope that is situated in ways to provide students with genuine and authentic learning opportunities, with such opportunities serving to springboard students' growth and development as well as achievement. Even more consequential is how these opportunities can help students to recognize the power that comes with enhanced degrees of their own civic-mindedness and democratic engagement.

Perhaps now more than ever, it is vital to rethink how teaching and learning occur in social studies classrooms. This is specific to social studies teachers because that speaks to the core of who I am—a former high school social studies teacher and baseball coach of thirteen years who now serves as a teacher educator. Where I would previously wax poetic on the various implications of the French Revolution, I now work tirelessly to help produce the best and brightest minds to go out and become the best professional educators they can be. Simply put—this writing is personal. One of my hopes, among other things, is that this work presents a passion that is clear and obvious—not just for the field but for all those wonderful young people with whom you have the pleasure to work.

Discussions and Democracy aims to support current and future social studies teachers in K-12 classrooms. While social studies is positioned to promote democratic practices, curricular pressures and educational reforms often steer to an overreliance on traditional and teacher-centered methods of instruction, causing students to learn with varying degrees of passivity. Moreover, such overreliance pushes teachers and students further away from the aims of social studies education that include promotion of civic competence "required of students to be active and engaged participants in public life" (NCSS, 2010).

Thus, authentic methods of instruction, such as discussion pedagogy, need to be explored to promote both the aim of social studies as well as student motivation and engagement. Discussion pedagogy, through seminars and deliberations, demonstrates the potential to

- reduce the gap between the rhetoric and the reality of social studies education;
- promote democratic education and civic-mindedness for students in social studies classrooms;
- support students' needs as they relate to student agency and autonomy in the educational process;
- facilitate students' intrinsic motivation through experiential learning environments;
- develop students' historical thinking skills; and
- enhance students' development of soft skills related to communication, critical thinking, and active listening.

The need for this type of work is evident as significant intersections exist among discussion pedagogy, democratic education, and student motivation. This is not a traditional textbook. As the challenges we face are new, so too must be how we approach them. Rather than lecturing to the audience, this book will guide you through a landscape of real-world examples and professional vignettes. The aim throughout is to bring important concepts and theories out of the "ivory tower" and onto the hard ground of real-world experience as a guide for today's social studies teachers.

It is written in a vernacular that will support teachers' understandings of implementing discussion-based approaches in their classrooms. Moreover, it drills down more deeply into student motivation and engagement. This is braided through a detailed and easy-to-understand explanation of self-determination theory (SDT). Understanding the principles of motivation in the teaching and learning process is essential to effective pedagogy.

This book can serve the needs of both new and experienced teachers interested in applying new methods of instruction to their already existing practice. It is written with teachers and students in mind—filled with specific steps and examples, as well as with problem-solving support for the challenges that might occur. In essence, this book is written by a teacher and is focused on teachers dedicated to their craft.

The journey begins with the history of social studies education and concludes with a hope that through meaningful instructional practices, our students will be motivated in the moment while also carrying with them the guiding principles related to civic competence and democratic mindedness. The more students are exposed to such practices, the greater the opportunity for them to serve as the bedrock for democracy to grow and flourish.

"The History" focuses on the turbulent history of social studies, which has been at the center of debate for well over a century. It is a narrative filled with misguided steps and reform efforts that, at times, have been intensified by the politics of the day. Several events were selected to serve as exemplars to illustrate the problems that have existed. The purpose of this chapter is to support teachers' understanding of the struggle that has existed. Moreover, the chapter finishes with the hopeful opportunities that could exist on the horizon. This awareness will allow teachers to be more apt to navigate and reconcile future problems when attempting to utilize authentic instructional methods.

"The Rhetoric and the Reality" delves into the aims and purposes of social studies education. It will help teachers make sense of how the aim of social studies education can be utilized to guide their instructional practices. The rhetoric is steeped in the promotion of supporting students developing civic competency and democratic mindedness. The unfortunate reality, in many cases, is filled with pressures that include curricular changes, standardized tests, and so on. As a result of such pressures, teachers have become over-reliant on traditional, teacher-centered methods. Direct instruction, while beneficial in certain times and spaces, needs to be supplemented with more authentic approaches. Approaches, such as discussion pedagogy, show tremendous potential to enhance classroom activity and engagement while also bridging the discord between the rhetoric and the reality.

"The Enlightenment" explores the utilization of seminars in social studies classrooms. Seminars are intended to create opportunities for enlightenment where students can explore meaningful texts that are couched in the development of a centralizing question. The development and implementation of seminars shift the focus of the classroom and create a de-centering of the teacher as the sole gatekeeper of information. In addition to describing the concepts and purposes related to seminars, this chapter will provide exemplars and suggestions for selecting meaningful texts and development of centralizing questions.

"The Deliberation" evaluates the impact of political engagement that can be experienced with deliberations. In comparison to seminars, deliberations are less about *knowing* and more about how students can reach a decision to commonly identified problems. Many deliberations take shape through structured academic controversies. While seminars and deliberations can be braided to create opportunities for *enlightened political engagement*, deliberations help students flesh out their powers of understanding while also attempting to make informed decisions—both democratically and dialectically.

"The Listening" focuses on an often-undervalued aspect of both seminars and deliberations—active listening. While students are expected to be active discussants, it is just as important that they understand the constructs surrounding being an active listener. Whether the purpose of the discussion is for knowing and/or political engagement, teachers and students will need to take pause to focus on listening strategies that will ultimately provide for the most fruitful discussions to take place. This chapter delineates concepts and actions that can be taught and learned to support discussion-based approaches in social studies classrooms.

"The Motivation" shifts gears to support teachers' understandings of what motivates and engages students. Describing motivational principles through SDT, this chapter helps teachers recognize how existing practices and behaviors can either promote or impede student motivation. Moreover, it will explain the differences between intrinsic and extrinsic motivation and how teachers' actions and behaviors can either support or thwart students' intrinsic motivation. This chapter is steeped in conceptual frameworks but is written in a fashion that will be welcoming to teachers—regardless of their baseline related to the theories.

"The Support" serves as an extension of chapter 6 in that it braids the conceptualizations of self-determination with the actionable behaviors of discussion pedagogy. To this end, this chapter will break down how discussion in classrooms can support students' innate psychological needs of autonomy, competence, and relatedness. Support of students' innate psychological needs with seminars and deliberations presents opportunities to create more democratic, or autonomy-supportive, learning environments. Thus, this chapter will demonstrate how discussion-based approaches can support students' needs and facilitate their intrinsic motivation, all while promoting characteristics related to democratic education.

"The Community" describes how discussion-based approaches support students' sense of relatedness to the teacher and to classmates as well as to the content. Students' participation in discussion-based approaches has shown to enhance students' comfort in social studies classes while also promoting nurturing interpersonal relationships. Additionally, through the lens of SDT and findings from action research studies, this chapter will illustrate how a community of learners can be developed.

"The Skills" focuses on a variety of skills students will need to develop as they move forward in their future lives. In addition to historical thinking skills, such as argumentation, discussion-based approaches show significant connections to the soft skills requisite in higher education and/or the professional workforce. These soft skills include the ability to effectively communicate, critically think, collaborate, and make informed decisions. The skills and characteristics associated with discussion pedagogy align with the soft skills students will need to operate in a diverse and interdependent democratic republic.

"The Change" crystallizes the previous chapters in order to display the change needed in schools. More importantly, it describes the pursuit of democratizing classrooms and how such a pursuit can impact our democracy moving forward. The actions and experiences affiliated with discussion pedagogy provide students with an opportunity to serve as active participants in their own educational processes. Processes, such as active discussion and active listening, in addition to opportunities for problem-solving, provide students with the tools required to serve as active participants in their future democratic lives.

While there is much that is grappled with throughout the book, each chapter is developed with the idea of helping social studies teachers to take a small bite of the apple each step of the way. As teachers, the class begins and ends with us. What happens in between must include your students. Thus, if you wish to act as an agent of change for and with your students, then there is no better time than now. While change is never easy, the hope is that this book will help you to support your students with the ability to think and process information critically. Ultimately, it seeks to help them live more effectively in a world where open discourse and the dialectic are becoming a lost skill.

Chapter 1

The History

Throughout the development of this book, I reflected often on my thirteen years as a social studies teacher and my nearly twenty years in education. Like many teachers, I had my go-to materials and activities that I would employ in my classes. For pre-service teachers reading this, as you might suspect, these are the activities that are tried-and-true and that seemingly always get the results for which we are hoping. The longer you are in the classroom, the more of these activities you will assuredly collect, and I had one such activity that I would use on the first day of class.

My goal for this exercise was twofold. First, I wanted students to realize that their ideas mattered and that their voices would be heard in my class. Second, I wanted them to analyze a selected reading that focused on the importance of studying history. The reading provided to students was Peter Stearns's 1998 article titled "Why Study History?"

Serving as a diagnostic assessment of sorts, I would ask students to pre-write about their thoughts and experiences in previous social studies courses. I would also ask them to draft ideas on why they believe they should study history (and the social studies at large). After completing the pre-writing, I supported students as they navigated a whole-group discussion by monitoring and redirecting where necessary—an exercise inextricably linked with the volleying of questions. Invariably, students would agree on one particular axiom regarding our reason for studying history, in that knowing history could help us prevent repeating mistakes of the past.

In concluding the opening portion of the exercise, students would then read Stearns's article and then be tasked with identifying at least one of the six arguments Stearns posits that resonated with them. The six points of emphasis included the following:

1. *History Helps Us Understand People and Societies.*
2. *History Helps Us Understand Change and How the Society We Live in Came to Be.*
3. *The Importance of History in Our Own Lives.*
4. *History Contributes to Moral Understanding.*
5. *History Provides Identity.*
6. *Studying History is Essential for Good Citizenship.*

This portion of the exercise was intended to promote the relevance of history in students' lives. As Stearns makes evident, history is all around us and provides us with opportunities to make meaning of ourselves and of others. Following their reading, another discussion would ensue. In the exchange of ideas that followed, students would often describe how the content and associated skills embedded within history and social studies classes could aid them in ways that they had never before considered. As a teacher, these are the moments for which we consistently strive.

Moreover, these moments, for me, were a testament to the cogency of Stearns's arguments. Stearns furthered his claims by identifying skills that could be gained from learning history and how those skills could aid them in their future academic and professional as personal lives. Those included the following:

1. *The Ability to Assess Evidence and Conflicting Interpretations.*
2. *Experience in Assessing Past Examples of Change.*
3. *History is Useful in the World of Work.*

Conversely, many students were quick to point out that those ideas and skills posited by Stearns were rarely, or not at all, reflective of their experiences in previous courses taken. Their candid reflections always troubled me. Students would tell descriptive tales of boring classes where dates and facts as well as historical figures were taught for later recitation on some type of test or quiz. It was as Wineburg (2018) describes as the familiar coziness associated with the "read-the-chapter-and-answer-the-questions-in-the-back-pedagogy" (p. 6).

This opening-day exercise always left me with questions about how exactly we had gotten to this point. In trying to isolate the cause(s), I would immediately turn to—and often deride—the most recent standards-based curricula that aligned with the increasing number of inundating end-of-the-year standardized exams. The one thing I did not realize, at least early in my career, was that the struggle for control of social studies education grossly pre-dated the standards and exams with which my colleagues, my students, and I were dealing.

While I wanted so badly to blame the current educational milieu and the decision-making stakeholders at the local, state, and federal levels, I eventually would come to learn that the saga of social studies education was much more of a spider web than I could have ever imagined. I believe that "knowing our history" is vitally important—so much so that I now spend the first couple of weeks in my social studies methods courses, helping both pre- and in-service students navigate and untangle aspects of that historical web.

Irrespective of professional experience, I believe a deeper understanding will help them to more positively impact their students' learning and understanding relative to all that social studies courses can potentially offer. While they get frustrated by what they learn in the prescribed readings, it is my hope that this knowledge will guide them in challenging future "shots" that will assuredly be fired at their chosen profession and field of study.

As you navigate this chapter, my hope is that you become keenly aware of the progress, missteps, and outright mistakes that have been made in the history of social studies education. Additionally, it is important for me to point out that I neither claim to be an educational historian nor do I believe that the "defining" moments I describe merit claim as an exhaustive list. Those defining moments I isolate throughout the remainder of the chapter are intended to be illustrative. As my introduction into the history of social studies education began as a doctoral student, those learning experiences have resonated with me as I now work with social studies teachers. To me, we need to know our history so that we can navigate current circumstances in the field.

CREATING AN UNDERSTANDING

The purpose of social studies has been, at times, difficult to recognize given its tumultuous history. This is a history steeped in a series of near-constant battles over what should be taught and to whom. In fact, these are battles that continue to linger to this day. Contextual circumstances and political agendas have led to social studies education being a focal point for reform efforts that have often been, to say the least, underwhelming relative to intended outcomes.

In order to understand our purpose as social studies teachers today, it is imperative to peel back the metaphoric onion of history—not necessarily to vilify the ideas or agendas of those who comprised the various competing camps that Evans (2006) identifies, and that I make note of below. Rather, we need to know the history so that it will help to inform our beliefs and decision-making relative to our current educational practices. While change seems to be one of the few constants in our profession, our understanding of the past will provide opportunities to more effectively operate within the constructs of the next politicallycharged amendments to our *why*.

Below is an overview of critical turning points in our history. The selected events described below are not comprehensive—nor are they intended to be. The intent is to provide exemplars that wax symbolic regarding the vacillation in the purpose and perception of social studies education. Additionally, the hope is that by describing these events, it will help current social studies teachers to adapt and, when necessary, challenge impending educational realities. The events outlined below include the following:

- *The 1916 Report on Social Studies* and "Problems of American Democracy"
- Creation of the National Council for the Social Studies
- The 1930s and the Rugg Textbook Controversy
- The 1960s, Bruner, Keller, and the Cold War
- Barth and Shermis and the Three Traditions
- The 1980s and *A Nation at Risk*
- Ravitch and Traditional History
- The Twenty-First Century, The C3 Framework, and the Inquiry Design Model

In conclusion, before beginning this journey down memory lane, this chapter is intended to help us recognize our history while also being hopeful about the possibilities ahead. At times, it might appear bleak, but there is confidence that, through a deeper understanding, we will be able to identify how genuine and authentic practices can be developed to further the needs of our students while also making substantive progress in our field.

The *1916 Report on Social Studies* and "Problems of American Democracy"

The term *social studies* first gained prominence in the midst of World War I with the presentation of the *1916 Report on Social Studies* by the Committee on Social Studies. This committee, which served as an arm of the Commission on the Reorganization of Secondary Education, was charged with developing a more modern approach to curricular guidelines for social studies. In this, the third report, it became clear that social studies would be uniquely identified by comparison to other subject areas. This differentiation was largely a result of its social aims predicated on an "operational philosophy . . . from components of numerous personal and theoretical influences" (Jorgensen, 2014, p. 10).

Both sides of the philosophical aisle were filled with competing viewpoints. On one side, stood gatekeepers who sought to (1) promote the natural conservatism of schools, (2) preserve the supremacy of specific subjects, and

(3) maintain history methods as a means of cultural promotion. Conversely, others called for a radical reorganization that would present content relatable to students' interests and that would more adequately serve their future lives. Concurrent to this reorganization would be the promotion of educators to "work boldly and without any timid reservation" (Nelson, 1994, p. 48).

More practically, this attempt to develop a more modern approach to curricular guidelines created a noticeable emphasis on geography and history in the middle grades and civics in the ninth grade. Perhaps, one of the most interesting aspects of the *1916 Report* was the promotion of a capstone course in the twelfth grade that would be referred to as "Problems of American Democracy—Economic, Social, and Political." Conceptually, this development stood firmly on the belief that such a course would more aptly serve the purposes of secondary schools; not simply that of a singular subject (Greenan, 1930). Its premise was to promote course development based on an amalgam of principles and topics within specific disciplines. The Committee on Social Studies proposed course development on the principles of not discarding

> one social science in favor of another, nor attempt to crowd the several social sciences into this year in abridged forms; but to study actual problems, or issues, or conditions, as they occur in life, and in their several aspects, political, economic, and sociological. These problems or issues will naturally vary from year to year, and from class to class, but they should be selected on the grounds (1) of their immediate interest to the class and (2) of the vital importance to society. (Nelson, 2014, p. 50)

Ultimately, as Lyberger (1983) explains, such a course would also provide meaningful and relevant opportunities for students to engage in topics associated with (1) life, (2) protection of life and property, (3) civic beauty, (4) wealth, and (5) charities, among others. The debate over the vision of social studies was not limited to courses developed in the likeness of "Problems of American Democracy." Increasing debate existed in volatile turf wars where particular philosophical camps developed based on contemporary issues ranging from the economy and war to funding and reform efforts (Evans, 2004). The work of the Committee on Social Studies would serve as a significant catalyst for future debate.

Creation of the National Council for the Social Studies (NCSS)

The creation of the NCSS was financially aided, in part, by the American Historical Association (AHA). The development of such an organization was brought about in an attempt to bring order to the field of social studies. Additionally, it was developed with the intent to "close the gap between social scientists and secondary school teachers and to reexamine knowledge within the disciplines in light of potential use in schools" (Nelson, 1995, p. 17).

One of the primary ways NCSS sought to quell some of the discontent and lingering issues in the field was through its attempt to create an acceptable definition for the social studies. The burgeoning definition "weathered a number of storms over the curriculum . . . but unfortunately failed to adequately defend and promote a vision of social studies as a strong alternative to traditional history and the social sciences" (Evans, 2004, p. 36). This inability, at least initially, to clearly define the field and its overarching purpose, created an atmosphere of relative uncertainty in the early 1920s. By some accounts of its history, the first fifteen years might best be described as "directionless."

While gratification was not instantaneous, NCSS began to gain traction with various groups, to include those in higher education. The nascent organization had to compete to be seen as an equal stakeholder with other more established groups, such as the National Education Association (NEA) and the AHA. By the early 1930s, NCSS hit the proverbial campaign trail. In doing so, its presence began to resonate with teachers. Its credibility also improved with "social scientists with more pronounced academic views and involvement" (Nelson, 1995, p. 17).

NCSS continued to struggle for "acceptance, membership, intellectual respect and a political voice" in the debate about curricular standards in schools (p. 17). As time went on, the direction and credibility of NCSS would continue to be called into question. This serves as a shining example of the vacillation that existed in the field in the early part of the twentieth century.

The 1930s and Rugg Textbook Controversy

The 1930s led millions of Americans to experience a time of near-unimaginable socioeconomic devastation. As a result of the Great Depression, such unprecedented times opened the floodgates for criticism associated with the use of fiscal policies that allowed for "unhealthy corporate and banking structures, an unsound foreign trade, much economic misinformation, and the bad distribution of income" (Zinn, 1999, p. 386). At the same time, there was increasing advocacy for closer connections to be made between history and the social sciences in schools. As a focal point of this debate, there was a growing desire to reassert history as the predominant force of social studies curricula in schools (Nash et al., 2000). In addition to developing a disciplinary hierarchy within social studies, there was a resurgence to develop social studies in a manner that would be "firmly grounded in a reformist and social activist stance reflective of the early years of the Great Depression and the New Deal" (p. 38). Ostensibly, these approaches led to remarkable and, at times, polemical stances among competing interest groups. It also led some to call for an approach to social studies that would be increasingly critical and analytically driven.

Harold Rugg, an educational reformer, became symbolic of such a reform-minded and critically active movement. Drawing from progressivist views, which posited that the human experience could be furthered through the advancement of various disciplines, Rugg became affiliated with the social reconstructionist movement—which believed that schools should serve as vehicles for social change. Rugg developed a series of avant-garde social studies textbooks that intended to make students increasingly aware of injustices in American society while also promoting them to become active participants in bringing about social change (Bagenstos, 1977; Boesenberg & Poland, 2001; Evans, 2007). The Rugg "curriculum" was developed around the construct of problem-based instruction.

In his multi-volume texts, Rugg attempted to create a balanced approach to presenting history through five themes which he referred to as "frontiers." Rugg's books drew the ire and criticism of many, leading him to be criticized and labeled as un-American. Such a label was likely exacerbated by the United States' involvement in World War II which led to heightened feelings of patriotism.

Standing in defense of his books, Rugg promoted an approach that would provide learning opportunities that would address, and even critique, topics such as the economy and its weaknesses, capitalism, and the inequity of wealth distribution, among others (Boesenberg & Poland, 2001). Ultimately, the premium placed on war-time American patriotism—coupled with the need for the assimilation of immigrant workers—led many large-scale and influential business organizations and publishers to disseminate anti-Rugg propaganda. Such ferocious attacks led to a series of macro *wars* that sought to denounce educational material perceived to be even remotely un-American.

The 1960s, Bruner, Keller, and the Cold War

Perceptions of being un-American exhibited even greater consequences as a result of the anti-communist movements that proliferated during the Cold War. The need to develop educational curricula that would, in many ways, promote American exceptionalism became a high priority for leaders in Washington, DC. This push was steeped in the seemingly unbridled competition between oppositional concepts—to include, good versus evil, democracy versus communism, the United States versus the Soviet Union.

The need for victory led to public education becoming the metaphoric launching pad that could lead the United States into victory against its adversaries. This resulted in the recognition that there was a need for a more knowledgeable human capital. Such a transformation in thought led to educational reforms that redirected attention, often allocated for mathematics and natural sciences, toward social studies (Johanningmeier, 2010).

Jerome Bruner, perhaps best known for his contributions to the field of cognitive psychology, sought to develop a set of precise principles that could be utilized in the development of curriculum. The diplomatic stirrings of the Cold War likely helped to facilitate the convening of Bruner and other theorists. Such attempts to redirect the social studies became more apparent with Charles Keller's (1961) article titled, "Needed: Revolution in the Social Studies."

Keller positioned that the field of social studies was in utter despair and that its praxis in the classroom was designed and implemented by unimaginative educators who were over-reliant on pedantic teaching methods. Keller went on to push for the eradication of the term "social studies" due to its ambiguous properties. Further, he wanted to apply Bruner-like principles to social studies similar to that of other disciplines (Evans, 2004).

Due to the existing crisis in the field, Hertzberg (1981) points out that the social studies received an influx of cash unlike any other time in its brief existence. The crisis was perpetuated by the continued inability to define the social studies; ultimately, this troubled its ability to gain universal acceptance of its role and application educationally. By 1963, the Brunerian approach continued to gain traction by attempting to use approaches that would create "junior" or "little league historians" (Evans, 2004).

By 1965, another reform effort would be built in an attempt to develop a "new social studies." This latest effort was partly in response to the work of Fenton and Good (1965), whose article promoted teaching history through a lens of historical problems and historical documents. Similar to other movements, the striking criticism was steeped in a lack of congruence between the rhetoric and the reality.

This apparent discord existed due in large part to ambiguity of curricular materials that would ultimately place even more rigorous demands on teachers. Arguably, one of the most disconcerting aspects of the "new social studies" movement was that the belief in, and application of, citizenship education was nullified, deemed tacit, or generally ignored (Hertzberg, 1981).

Barth and Shermis and the Three Traditions

In 1970, James Barth and Samuel Shermis wrote what has become a seminal piece describing the three traditions associated with social studies. In "Defining the Social Studies: An Exploration of the Three Traditions," they discuss the purpose of social studies within each of the traditions along with

- the need and ability to define the term "social studies";
- defining citizenship and its consistent acceptance in various definitions of social studies; and
- exploring how the three value-laden traditions seek to advance the definition.

The three traditions include citizenship transmission, social studies as a social science, and social studies as reflective inquiry (p. 744).

Social studies as citizen transmission is based on the notion that a set of predetermined concepts, values, and norms exist that can be categorized and taught in discrete manners. The supposition is that every person should individually hold the same values and beliefs as those held in regard by others. Further, the accepted traits and norms are to be put into action by individuals in their future lives. Barth and Shermis believed that transmission was comprised of a mixture of "description" and "persuasion."

Concerning description, teachers would be responsible for transmitting information on people, events, and phenomena that have been predetermined to be a necessity. This type of transmission would be implemented irrespective of the teacher's feelings or concerns on the topics. Persuasion serves to promote the underpinnings of a state's governmental political system as well as its social mores and values. This approach promotes that students should experience the feeling that progress is always good and righteous—irrespective of the cost. Thus, this approach leaves little to no room for interpretation. However, it does, in many ways, promote aspects of American exceptionalism throughout the curricular threads (pp. 744–746).

Social studies as a social science serves to make "amateur scholars" out of students through the use of methods utilized by academics and scholars. Topics and specific disciplines taught by scholars in higher education would then be teased out into simpler versions for students in K-12 spaces. As a social science, the purpose of gaining knowledge is simply that—gaining knowledge. Regarding citizenship, there exists a tacit assumption that by acquiring knowledge, there will be a natural and organic pathway toward "good citizenship."

The origins of reflective inquiry might date back to John Dewey, which was later summarized in Hunt and Metcalf's (1955) *Teaching High School Social Studies*. Unlike the other two traditions described, reflective inquiry proposes that methods in social studies should be utilized in an effort to *transform* students—not simply *transmit* information to students. With the promotion of citizenship and civic-mindedness serving as a cornerstone for social studies, it is important to address the role it plays in reflective inquiry. It must be believed that citizenship is a *process* and not simply *a collection of values* (p. 748).

Moreover, the decision-making process in citizenship should not be viewed as binary, meaning that because one item is good then the other is bad. In a classroom setting, the notion of decision-making and citizenship affords students the opportunity to make decisions "which affect them or are likely to affect them" (p. 749). These skills, which include making rational and cogent decisions after discussion and thought, are a critical component of daily living and proper citizenship in a democratic society.

The 1980s and *A Nation at Risk*

In 1981, President Ronald Reagan created the National Commission on Excellence in Education. Nearly two years later, the findings delivered from the committee was a report titled, *A Nation at Risk: The Imperative for Educational Reform*. The report, delivered by then-Secretary of Education Thomas Bell, reiterated a prominent claim since the mid-twentieth century the United States was falling behind its international counterparts as a result of diminishing human development. The report, similar to those that preceded it, reserved its most harsh criticism on schools for the mediocre students being produced—especially in an age where global competition was at a premium (Evans, 2004; Johanningmeier, 2010).

Social studies was mentioned three times in the report. The first mention concerned content recommendations and students. It was suggested that students seeking a high school diploma should take a minimum of three years of social studies. The second mention described how students should be able to do the following:

- Fix themselves and their futures within the "larger social and cultural contexts."
- Broadly understand "how ideas both ancient and contemporary shape the world."
- Understand the functionality of American economic and political systems.
- Differentiate "between free and repressive societies" (National Commission, 1983, pp. 21–22).

The third, and final mention, focused on the social studies as a critical component of the eight grades leading up to a student's secondary educational experience (p. 23).

Critics of the report called it out for being weak in its data and its faulty reporting of information. The arguments were based on inaccurate and misleading data that failed to capture the true and broader aims of education (Evans, 2004). Regardless of its potential inaccuracies, the report gained national attention with over 200,000 copies printed within five months of its presentation (Johanningmeier, 2010). Perhaps more importantly, it set the tone and the stage for additional political and educational posturing for the remainder of the 1980s, regarding schools and the educational model at large.

Ravitch and Traditional History

While her stances have dramatically shifted since the 1980s, educational historian Diane Ravitch set forth a line of questions and concerns regarding social studies education which would become prolific. The apparent inconsistencies in defining the social studies along with its ambiguity in orientation and curricular models allowed for Ravitch, Chester Finn, Paul Gagnon, and Lynne Cheney to call for a revival of history as an undeniable educational anchor. In fact, Ravitch and Finn's book (*What Do Our 17-Year-Olds Know?*) regarding the 1987 National Assessment of Educational Progress suggested, based on test scores, that students were "at risk of being gravely handicapped by . . . ignorance upon entry into adulthood, citizenship, and parenthood" (as cited in Wineburg, 2001).

Ravitch conjectured that history's position within the curriculum was dissipating as a result of having to share time with the "ill-defined" social studies curriculum (Evans, 2004). Funded by the conservative philanthropic Bradley Foundation, Ravitch and fellow historian Paul Gagnon reported that the social studies curriculum needed to take into account the necessity of making history relevant and meaningful to students. As imagined, the argument positioned by Ravitch and others, to sterilize the other disciplines contained within social studies for the sake of history, appeared to be nothing more than a scapegoat for some of the real issues of the time.

The Twenty-First Century, the C3 Framework, and the Inquiry Design Model

It should not be surprising that questions still abound regarding the role that social studies should play in the curricular nexus of our students' education. The fact that history education and social studies education continue to experience such a tenuous and uncomfortable relationship is somewhat perplexing and deliberative. The argument portrays these fields as two separate and, at times, diametrically opposing forces; however, in classroom practice, it is difficult to the see cause for battle lines to be drawn. As Lee (2005) suggests, "the commonalities are so extensive that often the terms . . . are used interchangeably or in tandem" (p. 61).

It is clear to see continuing changes remain with more likely on the horizon. This is notable given the significant changes in many state standards as it relates to social studies education. Much change is being focused on the purpose of social studies education and how content can be approached to enhance students' learning experiences through more constructivist approaches. As such, we need to look no further than developments and, in many cases, the acceptance of the C3 Framework and Inquiry Arc.

The C3 Framework and Inquiry Arc focus on the teaching and learning of social studies that intend to support students for their college, career, and civic lives. The C3 Framework was developed by various stakeholders, ranging from state agencies and organizations associated with social studies education as well as scholars in specific disciplines of study. Furthermore, the C3 Framework is centered on an Inquiry Arc where a set of intersecting and "mutually supportive ideas [sic] frame the ways students learn social studies content" (NCSS, 2013, p. 6).

At the heart of this endeavor was the recognition that students need the opportunity to develop and utilize deeper understandings related to society's problems while being able to develop and investigate proposed questions. Moreover, the C3 Framework is guided by several principles that comprise high-quality social studies education, including the following:

- The social studies prepare the nation's young people for success in college and career as well as informed, engaged participation in civic life.
- Inquiry is at the heart of social studies instruction.
- The social studies involve interdisciplinary instruction and benefit from interaction with and integration of the arts and humanities.
- The social studies is composed of deep and enduring understandings, concepts, and skills. Social studies emphasize skills and practices that prepare students for informed and engaged participation in civic life (Swan, 2013).

However, the investigation of probing questions does not end there. C3 supports and promotes that students learn how to effectively act upon what they learn after their development of fundamentally sound evidence-based claims and arguments. The painstaking work of stakeholders on this project has led, as an exemplar, to the development of the Inquiry Design Model (IDM).

Based on the work of John Lee, Kathy Swan, and S. G. Grant, IDM presents a refined instructional framework to support teachers and students as they engage in meaningful inquiries. IDM "is a distinctive approach to creating curriculum and instructional materials that honor teachers' knowledge and expertise, avoids over-prescription, and focuses the central elements of the instructional design process as envisioned in the Inquiry Arc" (Grant et al., 2015, p. 1).

One of the key aspects of the IDM is that teachers and students are provided opportunities to collaborate in constructivist-led exercises that will help prepare students for their current and future lives. Further, the application of such an approach—in a supplemental manner—aids in lessening of learning environments that are overly reliant on teacher-centered, stand-and-deliver methods of instruction. This approach begins with a rich and relevant question that students will navigate through the use of meaningful and varying source material. The intended objective is to help students at all grade levels develop evidence-based arguments that can be acted upon.

In de-centering the teacher in the classroom through engagements in such activities, students are afforded the opportunity to exercise agency and autonomy in their own learning. Frameworks such as C3 and IDM are helping to pave the way for other instructional methods to be further explored by decision-making stakeholders. In essence, this provides hope in the sense that teachers very well might be on the precipice of being honored for their content and pedagogical knowledge while students will be pushed to be more than the passive recipients of content that would be stored for later recitation.

FINAL THOUGHTS

While hope might be on the horizon for teachers and their students, it will be imperative for us to continue to explore additional opportunities for meaningful and authentic engagement. To that end, this has become the purpose of writing this book. As will be evaluated in the subsequent chapters, I want to closely evaluate the promotion of discussion pedagogy—with its seminars and deliberations—that serves our students in ways that create agency and activity for our students.

Additionally, this book will periodically review how systematic implementation of discussion-based approaches can also help to achieve the goals of those from our past. This includes Rugg's push for problem-based instruction and Barth and Shermis' belief that social studies can aid in student transformation through reflective inquiry, among others.

What makes this endeavor unique is the intersection that this book intends to create between the social studies and motivational theories in the field of educational psychology. Through the lens of self-determination theory (SDT), we will discover the myriad, observable benefits that could exist with the thoughtful implementation of discussion-based approaches. Moreover, there will be attempts made to share how such implementation could get us back to our True North while reducing the gross disparity between the rhetoric and reality of social studies education—as it still exists today.

Chapter 2

The Rhetoric and the Reality

Evidence exists that there is a continued need to explore the aim of social studies education. The tumultuous past illustrated in the first chapter could send anyone into a dizzying tailspin. Admittedly, I was several years into my career before I became keenly aware of the aim. What became apparent was that what I believed my purpose to be was not always aligned with that aim and its characteristics.

First, I believed that one of my primary purposes was to help my students identify and utilize techniques that would help them to be better learners—in my class as well as in others. This neatly aligned with available scholarship that posits that all teachers, irrespective of the content area, are teachers of reading, writing, thinking, and study skills (Carjuzaa & Kellough, 2016). Second, I always felt a sense that guiding students toward an appreciation of the content being learned was important to their overall learning experience. At the beginning of each semester, I would unabashedly promulgate to my students that they would find at least one topic that genuinely intrigued and challenged them. Distilled down, these two purposes encompassed a belief that I could help grow my students while allowing them to gain an appreciation for the social studies.[1]

I believe my roles and my purposes were sound, thoughtful, and concerned about the well-being of my students. That being said, it was not until I was a first-year doctoral student that it became abundantly clear that I did not fully grasp the actual aim of social studies education at large. Quite frankly, once I did, it kind of shook me. This immediately led me to reflect on my pedagogical philosophy as well as on my instructional designs and methods. Through that reflection, which was incredibly humbling, I realized that I was not doing enough and that my methods were not going far enough. All of this is to say that I wholeheartedly believe that both pre- and in-service social studies teachers need to flesh out how their respective roles and purposes align and intersect with the aim of social studies education.

What I felt about my own practices might be something some of you might have experienced or even might experience in your future practice. This disconnect is what I have often referred to as the discord between the "rhetoric and the reality" of social studies education. The rhetoric, steeped in pedagogically sound characteristics and achievable goals for promoting democratic citizenship and civic engagement, is often thwarted by the reality of impediments and pressures that both teachers and students experience on a daily basis.

THE RHETORIC

In digging through the works of well-recognized scholars in the field, most are in concert related to the purpose of social studies education. Through multiple iterations positioned by the National Council for the Social Studies (NCSS), one thing has remained steady as it relates to the purpose—a commitment to promoting civic competence. In 2010, as part of The National Curriculum Standards, NCSS defined the aim of social studies as "the promotion of civic competence—the knowledge, intellectual process, and democratic dispositions required of students to be active and engaged participants in public life" (p. 9).

While mostly in lockstep, there remains a desire by NCSS to revise and amend the purposes and disciplines that define the field. As recently as June 2023, an email was sent out to stakeholders in the field regarding a potential revision to the definition of social studies that dates back to 1994. NCSS proposed a recommended change for the definition of social studies to be as follows: "Social Studies is the study of individuals, people, and communities through time and place by analyzing evidence from multiple sources" (NCSS, personal communication, June 1, 2023).

Additionally, a draft of recommended changes related to the purpose of social studies included, "Social Studies helps students to navigate the world. By exploring the past, participating in the present, and looking toward the future, Social Studies prepares learners for life-long practice of civil discourse and civic engagement in their communities and the world" (NCSS, 2023). Two things that stand out about the proposed revisions are that there continues to be a steady push for civic-mindedness and engagement with an emphasis on civil discourse.

Thus, social studies coursework should be filled with opportunities where students learn the processes associated with civic competence that will aid them in becoming active agents for informed and reasoned decision-making.

NCSS (2010) unpacks "civic competence" further by describing that it "rests on [the] commitment to democratic values, and requires the abilities to use knowledge about one's community nation, and world; apply inquiry process; and employ skills of data collection and analysis, collaboration, decision-making, and problem-solving" (p. 9).

Pursuit of such powerful teaching and learning opportunities in social studies might appear somewhat overwhelming, especially given all the hats that teachers are expected to wear daily. When the above aspects are distilled and compartmentalized, it is more than likely that existing practices in your classes hit on many of these aspects—both routinely and thoughtfully. The challenge is how to push our practices, and concurrently our students, even further toward being democratically minded and civically engaged. This push will allow us to broaden opportunities for critical thinking, piqued curiosity, and intellectual engagement along with the aim of social studies education.

Commitment to Democratic Values and Citizenship

Striving toward democratic education has the potential to avail in the development of learning environments where teachers and students work *with* one another in transformative and meaningful ways. Democratic education encourages students to develop initiative and imagination where teachers' instructional foci is shifted from production to process-orientation. Democratic education is a "form of civic education that purposely teaches young people how to *do* democracy [which] stands at the crossroads of authenticity and transformation" (Hess, 2009, p. 15). This means, in continuing this journey, it is important to keep in mind that social studies education must be built for citizenship, participation, and engagement. Hold these ideas close because the path to progress will not always be linear.

This certainly holds true when it comes to concepts surrounding democratic citizenship as a defining characteristic for social studies. The problem in this case is enveloped in the difficulty in defining what democratic citizenship means. The apparent Janus-like characteristics relative to the ideals of democracy tend to create enhanced levels of ambiguity. When utilizing the phrase *ideals of democracy*, there is the implication that every human being is of immeasurable worth, is of infinite value, is a creative force, and is deserving of unqualified respect (Ayers et al., 2010). Democracy is a contested concept that is marked by continual debate because its meaning is steeped in sociocultural and political contexts (Parker, 1996).

The concept is positioned along two ideological extremes. One end is situated in a revisionist perspective that seeks to challenge and resist every aspect of oppression that is antithetical to democratic ideals. Ideologically, in this extreme case, true democracy attempts to disrupt and resist "all forms and systems of oppression" (McKnight & Chandler, 2009, p. 60).

The other, more conservative in its ideals, supports the sociopolitical status quo, where unquestioned support is given to our chosen leaders. This dialectical tension ultimately creates issues for teachers seeking to develop their students' awareness of, and potential for, action as it relates to democratic citizenship and civic engagement. Another perspective from Parker (2001) contends that teachers and students should engage and understand aspects related to liberty and pluralism as well as the rule of law and citizen rights. This includes the learning that "abhor[s] demagoguery, discrimination, oppressions, and military rule" (p. 6).

While definitional tensions clearly exist related to democratic citizenship and social studies, there are still aspects of the aim for social studies education that can be used as a springboard. While writing about these opportunities with hope and conviction, there is also a reality that teachers and students do not teach and learn in a vacuum. There are numerous constraints placed on the teaching and learning process that can thwart progress toward our purpose and movement in the proper direction of the aim of social studies. These impediments are aplenty and can, at times, create a sense of helplessness for all involved. Despite the potential trepidation, it is vitally important to stay the course.

THE REALITY

In reading the aim and the characteristics of social studies, images might begin to populate. These images might include classrooms filled with students who are engaged and excited with their learning experiences of which they are a part. There is no doubt that an unbridled desire exists to have students actively participating in your classes in ways that demonstrate growth in their critical thinking while also understanding how such knowledge can impact their future lives. Assuredly, there is also a want to facilitate those *aha* moments where students exude a genuine curiosity—whether it be a result of the content and/or our instructional practices. These oft-sought-after moments as teachers are symbolic of good teaching that permeates the walls of classrooms and schools. Ultimately, it provides hope for the future.

For citizenship development in social studies classes to occur more routinely, students need to be afforded the time and the latitude to interpret topics—past and present—as well as make decisions in the classroom setting (Engle, 2003; Parker, 2006). Far too often, however, the *reality* of teaching and learning in social studies classrooms across the country looks very different because far too many students are being "socialized for adult civic life . . . in ways that are anything but democratic" (McQuillan, 2005, p. 639).

Distilled down, this means that social studies education has become a revolving door of simple *transmission* of accepted knowledge provided to students. This means that students are not provided enough authentic opportunities to *transform* accepted knowledge for the purpose of serving as civic-minded active participants in their educational experiences or their democratic lives. Culpability for this discord between the rhetoric and the reality should never fall solely on the shoulders of teachers nor their students—although it often does.

There are numerous challenges evident that thwart even more of these moments from occurring regularly, making it necessary for further exploration of how the educational milieu might impede the promotion of democratic citizenship and civic engagement. In part, this is resultant of the various pressures that impact both teachers and students.

Stanley (2005) suggests that given "our cultural commitment in the United States to individualism and free market theory, the limited impact of education for social transformation should not be surprising" (p. 282). The paradox of promoting democratic citizenship in traditionally conservative settings provides evidence that contemporary societal values are taking priority over the consistent philosophical underpinnings of citizenship, as perceived to be a cornerstone of social studies. Moreover, extant pressures (e.g., community, charged agencies and policy, standards and accountability measures, etc.) make it difficult for schools (and teachers) to do anything more than transmit the status quo (Stanley, 2005; Giroux, 2001).

Perhaps, unlike other fields of study such as those disciplines within the *hard* sciences and mathematics, social studies has an incredibly unique relevance that can be experienced through courses such as history, geography, psychology, sociology, and political science, among others. This unique relevance places social studies in a premium position to promote democratic citizenship. In his seminal piece, *Democracy and Education*, John Dewey (1916) suggests that for meaning to exist, experiences must be real in nature to students. Thus, the more human and open the experience (i.e., democratic), the more real the experience will be relative to real knowledge.

If the research shares that meaningful learning requires meaningful experience, then why does such a disconnect exist? In part, it is a result of schools, like other institutions, operating in such a hierarchical system where teachers and students are marginalized in the educational process. A lack of consensus exists regarding the cause of disparity, whether it is a result of curricula, pedagogies, and/or policies (Kumashiro, 2000). Much discussion has been made about the intensification, de-skilling and proletarianization of teachers and their role as intellectuals (Apple, 2009; Giroux, 1988).

Like teachers, students are often marginalized participants in the supposed democratic, educational process. This marginalization exists within the power structure of classrooms and school buildings where students' respective *voices* are not heard, often because their beliefs are perceived to be unsolicited and/or irrelevant. The marginalization of students in social studies classrooms, or any classroom for that matter, does not serve the long-term interests of students as participants in classroom settings; more importantly, it does not serve their interests toward becoming active citizens in a democratic state. For democratic citizenship to be realistically achieved, teachers and students need to be able to think openly and question as well as imagine the alternatives that are possible (Ayers et al., 2010).

Thus, in order for democratic citizenship to serve as a functional purpose for social studies, it is necessary to allow teachers to serve as transformative intellectuals, "who combine scholarly reflection and practice in the service of educating students to be thoughtful, active citizens" (Giroux, 1985, p. 376). Allowing for more open and public thought as well as democratic discourse in schools should be viewed as being aligned with a democratic society; the basic underpinnings of a democracy should promote openness, participation, and equity as well as inquiry, among others (Ayers et al., 2009; Parker, 2006, 1997).

Testing, Restraints, and Overreliance

A part of the *de-skilling* of teachers comes from the often-restrictive standards created by state and federal agencies that are often coupled with high-stakes, standardized exams. These overwhelming standardized measures have consequences for teachers if performance expectations are not met to the degree prescribed. This intensification of the teaching process, as Apple (2009) describes, has led to outside influences gaining increasing control over daily classroom practices. It is possible that many teachers would agree that solely using standardized tests only scratches the surface toward truly assessing the educational health and well-being of schools and their students.

Of course, this actually calls into question what it means to say a school is doing well—especially when "too few policymakers have ever taught in public schools" (Eisner & Cuban, 2013, p. 1). To be clear, standards are a necessity to effectively guide both teachers and students in the classroom. Make note of the term *necessity* and do not let that be remotely confused with *necessary evil*. Learning how to read and navigate state and national standards as part of the instructional planning process is a vital part of learning how to effectively teach. It is necessary to understand what needs to be taught and what "concepts and skills should be developed," making this part of the standard operating procedure when working through the instructional design process (Beal & Bolick, 2013, p. 69).

The standards movement, however, became less about focusing on the teaching and learning process and more about accountability. Eisner (2001) writes,

> The formulation of standards and the measurement of performance were intended to tidy up a messy system and to make teachers and schools administrators truly accountable. The aim was . . . to systematize and standardize so that the public will know which schools are performing well and which are not. There were to be . . . payments and penalties for performance. (p. 367)

Too often, instead of analyzing the techniques associated with evaluating teachers and students (i.e., standardized testing), pressure is placed solely on schools, teachers, and students to make the appropriate corrections in the teaching and learning process. In doing so, more reform efforts and recalibrated standards get pushed through the pipeline and thrown into the laps of teachers to make sense of. This creates a pattern of meaningless lip service veiled as an attempt to make this generation of students better and more knowledgeable. Going back to the evaluation of assessment techniques, Wineburg (2018) elucidates that students "look dumb on history tests because the system conspires to make them look dumb. The system's rigged. As practiced by the big testing companies, modern psychometrics guarantees that test results will conform to a symmetrical bell curve" (p. 16).

With payments and penalties looming, it creates a sense of pressure that teachers experience—from above, from within, and from below. The pressure experienced by teachers is typically manifested through the development of instructional practices that would be best described as teacher-centric and controlling-motivating. As a result, many teachers tend to adopt practices that have lingered far too long in our instructional toolboxes—transmission of information/accepted knowledge through stand-and-deliver techniques.

This has numerous consequences, which include reducing the aim of character development and good citizenship in order to increase transmission of information and basic knowledge acquisition (Engle, 2003). To be clear, direct instruction certainly has merit as a productive method for instruction, so long as it is not the predominant method of instructional delivery.

For a moment, let us revisit the aim of social studies education. It speaks to the promotion of democratic citizenship and civic engagement based on characteristics that include opportunities for inquiry, collaboration, decision-making, and analysis. Overutilizing strategies whetted to teachers acting as the sage on the stage does not promote any of those characteristics associated with the aim of social studies education.

Earlier in the chapter, I described my identified purposes which included improving my students' skills while also helping them to gain greater appreciation for the content. To accomplish these purposes, there was a great deal of lecturing coupled with a systematic volleying of questions and opportunities for practice and rehearsal. Such practices were intended to support students' cognitive needs and shortcomings while also supporting all students for future learning environments, including post-secondary opportunities.

For those students who planned on going to a two- or four-year institution upon graduation, there was a particular belief that they were going to have to learn how to listen to professors during classes while they feverishly took notes. That was my experience in college. Thus, the lectures would support their respective abilities to have the same experience and be successful. A gap in understanding of the rhetoric related to social studies education early in my career kept me in the dark that other instructional methods could truly avail my students in much more important ways. In the moment, however, there was also failure to realize that my methods were creating other unintended consequences for my students.

Looking back, the first and most obvious consequence was the perpetuation of the "banking" concept of teaching and learning. Paulo Freire, a Brazilian educator and philosopher best known for his work, *Pedagogy of the Oppressed*, describes traditional educational systems in which students behave as the passive receivers of information where memorization, and subsequent recitation, reigns supreme. Freire (2014) contended,

> Education thus becomes an act of depositing, in which the students are the depositories and the teacher is the depositor. . . . This is the "banking" concept of education, in which the scope of action allowed to the students extends only as far as receiving, filing, and storing the deposits. They do, it is true, have the opportunity to become collectors or cataloguers of the things they store. But in the last analysis, it is the people themselves who are filed away through the lack of creativity, transformation, and knowledge in this (at best) misguided system. (p. 72)

While the use of directive practices can be validated by the benefits they produce, it is important to see that, like with most things in life, too much of any one thing is usually harmful. There is another takeaway from Freire's work regarding the overreliance of direct instruction. Not only does it not support the aim and characteristics of social studies education, it also creates a tacit hierarchy within classrooms. Do not misunderstand; teachers must have classroom management strategies, with their rules and consequences as well as procedures, developed well in advance to make any class run smoothly.

There is no suggestion here that hierarchies should not exist in terms of managing a classroom. The hierarchy being described concerns teaching *to* students instead of learning *with* students. The division created by the overreliance of direct instruction develops a noticeable dichotomy in our classes. Such overreliance leads to a banking concept based on unidirectional learning environments, where

1. the teacher teaches and the students are taught;
2. the teacher knows everything and the students know nothing;
3. the teacher talks and the students listen;
4. the teacher chooses and enforces his or her choice, and the students comply; and
5. the teacher is the subject of the learning process, while pupils are the mere objects (Freire, 2014).

In addition to suppressing students' agency in their own education, it also leads to a potential where students will become increasingly apathetic to learning in general. It prevents them from engaging in critical-thinking opportunities as a result of the "passive role imposed on them" (Freire, 2014). Student apathy in the classroom can lead to a panoply of issues, both instructionally and in terms of management.

The second unintended consequence is that classrooms are developed via controlling-motivating means. Finding ways to facilitate our students' motivation is an undeniably important facet of the job. As will be addressed in a later chapter, there is a significant difference between utilizing instructional methods that are autonomy-supportive versus controlling-motivating. In addition to creating an environment based on the banking concept, we are also promoting learning environments that are controlling-motivating.

The use of any one of the following approaches to motivate students is controlling-motivating in nature: (1) adopt only the teacher's perspective; (2) intrude into students' thoughts, feelings, or actions; and (3) pressure students to think, feel, or behave in particular ways (Reeve, 2009). Simply put, controlling-motivating methods of instruction have proven to negatively impact the climate of learning environments which can lead to students' intrinsic motivation and self-esteem being frustrated (Deci & Ryan, 1982). It also leads teachers to over-exercise external controls, such as rewards and punishments, as measures to ensure that learning is taking place. The end result is that too many students respond to their learning environment with boredom coupled with feelings of alienation (Niemec & Ryan, 2009).

There is a difference between balanced implementation and overreliance on direct instruction. A heightened self-awareness about practices being utilized is a first step toward moving along that linear path toward progress.

Direct instruction can benefit students and the overall learning environment. However, as Carjuzaa and Kellough (2016) point out, "this one-directional concept with delivery mode assumes that a student is a tabula rasa (blank state)" (p. 256). Thus, a balance of instructional methods must be developed in order to develop our students in ways that aid us in reaching our larger purpose.

It is also evident that such an overreliance does little to promote students' opportunities to genuinely engage with, and explore, the prescribed content and standards. Students are the ones who get lost in the curriculum, the standards, and the purpose. Thus, it becomes a pedagogical imperative to identify and utilize authentic methods of instruction that have the potential to bring students closer to forming their understandings of civic responsibilities and democratic citizenship.

In addition to utilizing direct (delivery) modes of instruction, balanced alternative approaches need to be addressed by way of access modes of delivery. Access modes of delivery "provide students with access to information by working *with* students" (p. 256). Such strategies include learning that is predicated on (1) cooperation, (2) problem- and project-based approaches, (3) inquiry, and (4) discussion pedagogy. Access modes promote constructivist-based approaches that show greater potential to promote student agency and autonomy. Ultimately, a balanced approach of both delivery and access modes—with their respective strengths and weaknesses (see table 2.1)—will help reduce the gap between the rhetoric and the reality.

Table 2.1 Strengths and Weakness of Delivery and Access Modes

Mode	Strengths	Weaknesses
Delivery	• Increased content coverage in limited time frame • Teacher control of content coverage • Strategies associated with delivery mode support competency-based instruction • Student achievement is predictable and manageable	• Student motivation is mostly extrinsic • Students make few important decisions about their learning • Limited opportunity for creative or divergent thinking • Student self-esteem might be inadequately served
Access	• Students learn the content more in-depth • Student motivation is more likely intrinsic • Students have more control over the pacing • Students can serve as educational decision-makers	• Content coverage might be limited • Strategies can be time-consuming • The teacher has less control over time • The specific results of student learning are less predictable

Source: Adapted from Carjuzaa and Kellough (2016).

FINAL THOUGHTS

This might be a good place to do some unpacking. Throughout this unpacking process, there is a term that my methods students have grown to love and hate—congruent. Not to worry, there is no math lesson to follow. In definitional terms, congruent, when used as an adjective, suggests there is an existence of agreement or harmony. To be effective teachers *with* students, there are variables that need to be congruent. When discussing the processes related to instructional planning, my students and I work together to make sure that existing standards are congruent with instructional objectives which, in turn, need to be congruent with instructional activities and assessments.

In this case, the term "congruent" will be used both conceptually and practically. Conceptually, our aim is to promote and support students as they become more engaged democratically and civically. Almost immediately, the rhetoric is thwarted by the more practical reality that extant pressures, to include standardized testing and curricular restraints, can create a lack of congruence in our classrooms. As a result of such pressures, there is a tendency to over-rely on methods such as direct instruction that can mitigate the breadth-depth paradox being experienced. Of course, this mitigation creates other patterns of incongruence to this kind of teaching versus the kind of learning desired for our students.

Looking forward to the exploration of other possibilities, it is clear that the systematic implementation of discussion pedagogy—with its seminars and deliberations—can serve as a conduit to getting our classes moving in a more linear and congruent path. The use of purposeful classroom discussion can authentically promote civic life where students experience a "culture of listening and speaking" to others who are similar and different from themselves which can serve the fundamental underpinnings of democratic life (Parker, 2006, p. 13).

While there has been extensive research on this topic by some of the best scholars in the field, this book intends to add an extra layer to the existing scholarship—concepts associated with motivation. In addition to exploring the tenets of discussion pedagogy and how it can mitigate the discord between the rhetoric and the reality, this book will flesh out how such approaches can help facilitate students' intrinsic motivation while supporting their needs. The term *needs* is a discrete reference to the support of students' psychological needs of autonomy, competence, and relatedness. The next chapter starts our collective pursuit toward a more linear progress that will benefit all of us—now and in the future.

NOTE

1. As an aside, a few years ago during Teacher Appreciation Week, I reposted a question from my friend and former colleague to social media, asking former students to fill me in on their lives while also sharing a story from our time together. I received over 300 responses, with many of them recalling their memories of learning about the finer points of the French Revolution. Thus, if nothing else, my second purpose might have been achieved.

Chapter 3

The Enlightenment

Discussions have powerful potential. I realized their potential about halfway through an action research study I was conducting on my own instructional methods with two of my courses. The premise was to develop and implement a systematic discussion-based intervention, leading me to modify my already existing practices. Thus, in lieu of being reliant on directive practices, I wanted to explore the implications of making classroom discussions an instructional staple.

The challenge was real. I had to retrain nearly a decade of instructional automaticity. Identifying and evaluating the best resources to utilize, coupled with creating intellectually challenging and engaging questions, was a months-long effort. Following what I believed to be a very thoughtful instructional redesign, I began by explaining the rationale for the changes to students. To me, providing them with the rationale for the intervention was tantamount to our collective collaboration and success. Implementation began, and quite frankly, it was better than I could have ever imagined. It was not without its flaws, but the students immediately took to it.

About halfway through the intervention, I experienced a kind of watershed moment. It was a Friday, and my students and I were working through content concerning the impacts of nationalism in the late nineteenth century. We had already worked through the impacts of nationalism as arguably the most powerful political ideology of the nineteenth century. We created meaningful intersections between nationalism and the beliefs and actions associated with imperial activities of the same period.

The discussion for that given day was anchored in a speech from former German chancellor Bernhard von Bülow titled "Hammer or Anvil" that was presented to the Reichstag in 1899. It is a powerful speech filled with intense rhetoric that sought, among other things, to promote German nationalism equal to, or greater than, their European counterparts. It was a speech that was emblematic of rampant and unchecked nationalism that ran wild. Going into this seminar, my confidence was brimming, and I just knew that students would use this, and other sources provided, to springboard themselves toward another thoughtful and productive discussion.

The confidence previously mentioned was immediately put in check. My students' lack of involvement and enthusiasm was coupled with moments of dreaded awkward silence that we have all experienced at one point or another in our classes. I could feel myself getting anxious and quite red in the face. Taking a deep breath, I attempted to subtly reframe the initial centralizing question. The silence remained deafening. I calmly prompted students by assuring them that it was okay to participate when they were ready, and I gave them a few more minutes to review their findings from the readings.

My heart steadily raced until a few moments later, when one of my students decided to speak. It was not the fact that someone took that first step; it was more about the student who chose to take that leap of faith. This was a student whom I had in two previous classes. She was quite shy and reserved in her demeanor. In fact, she had not yet outwardly participated in any of our discussions up to that point. Her response to the question was thoughtful and well-considered, and quite frankly, took everyone by surprise.

Following her remarks, the seminar ramped up, and we were once again in full swing. As the students discussed their beliefs and provided analysis based on their readings, I wrote the word "why" in my field notes. That one word served as a reminder that I wanted to know why that quiet and reserved student chose, at that most instructionally awkward of moments, to participate. More to come on that later, I promise.

I write all of this to say that no matter how well-developed and thoughtful the design of our instructional activities, there will be those moments of awkward silence and student reluctance. What is even more important, however, is that opportunities exist for students to speak freely and candidly as part of student-driven discussions. They have the potential to lead to moments that you and your students will likely never forget. They provide opportunities for moments of open discourse that are boundless in potential—where ultimately, students' opinions and feelings are valued and appreciated. In addition, it helps us to move ever closer toward our aim as social studies teachers.

CONCEPTUAL OVERVIEW AND PURPOSE

This book is written to support pre- and in-service social studies teachers; thus, it is important to stipulate that authentic approaches, such as discussion pedagogy—with its seminars and deliberations—should be considered in an effort to *enhance* already existing practices. This point is positioned front and center because, far too often, teachers are told that their practices need a total overhaul to meet the latest curricular trends, fads, or expectations. Discussion pedagogy should be viewed as another instructional tool that can be routinely utilized to support students.

Discussion pedagogy is a student-centered instructional method that can, and should, be implemented in all K-12 social studies classrooms. Development and implementation of discussion-based approaches present opportunities to move closer toward the aim of social studies education while also satisfying curricular requirements. Even greater, it demonstrates the potential to democratically enlighten and politically engage students while leading to the creation of learning environments that promote active student participation over mere recitation (Parker, 2004, 2006, 2010). It also demonstrates unique intersections toward the promotion of students' psychological needs and motivation.

While many teachers might believe that such discussions are already happening in their classes, this belief is often based on a practice of volleying questions that is then coupled with other interactive dialogue. This belief typically creates a disconnect because of teachers' misaligned conceptual understanding of what discussion-based approaches entail. While volleying questions can act as an important diagnostic and/or formative checkpoint, these actions are more akin to recitative practices. Classroom discussions "must involve a purposeful exchange of views—a dialogue—among the participants themselves" (Parker, 2001, p. 111). In fact, both seminars and deliberations support "purposeful discussion, as distinct from 'bull sessions,' which, though convivial, have no particular instructional purpose" (Parker, 2006, p. 12).

Purposeful classroom discussion demonstrates opportunities to authentically promote civic life where students can experience a "culture of listening and speaking" to others who are similar to, and different from, themselves. In addition to being pedagogically sound, it also serves as a fundamental underpinning of democratic life (Parker, 2006). Through seminars and deliberations, students will be given moments to change the landscape of dialogue in the classroom. Previous descriptions of teacher-student interactions had questions being transmitted to students by teachers with answers being returned to the teacher—thus concluding the restricted exchange. The types of seminars and deliberations that can be developed will likely create a much more varied and elastic series of opportunities.

Seminars give students opportunities to dive meaningfully into challenging texts coupled with centralizing questions. When seminars are used for the purpose of enlightenment, or *knowing*, students will serve as both active discussants and active listeners. Deliberations can be utilized for the purpose of political engagement, or *doing*. While seminars and deliberations characteristically overlap, deliberations are not necessarily intended for learning as much as they should focus on decision-making related to a shared problem (Parker, 2006). The overlap and use of each discourse has the potential to create *enlightened political engagement* (Parker, 2003, 2006).

Because seminars and deliberations will likely promote experiences characterized as knowledge-deepening and evidence-oriented, it also presents moments for a reduction in the use of authoritarian and teacher-centered classrooms. In essence, it de-centers the teacher as the gatekeeper of knowledge and re-centers the students as active agents in their own learning process. Teacher-dominated learning environments show stronger than normal relationships to lower student achievement as well as increased student anxiety and dependence (Stefanou et al., 2004).

Conversely, more democratic, or autonomy-supportive, environments enable students to seek out more challenging work and increase student enjoyment—all while supporting students who strive toward deeper conceptual understanding. Thus, the freedom to express thought and opinion can produce learning environments where students' engagement and interests can be fostered. Such environments can also encourage student initiative and nurture students' competency (Lipstein & Renninger, 2007; Parker, 2001; Stefanou et al., 2004).

Systematic implementation of seminars should be looked at as "a powerful way to engage students in historical, democratic, and ethical reasoning" (Kohlmeier, 2022, p. 63). Using terms like *systematic* and *strategic* is intentional because all instructional planning needs to be such—irrespective of what methods will be implemented. One thing that makes using discussions in social studies classes unique is the variation of outcomes that can occur. Walter Parker and Diana Hess (2001), both leading scholars in

Table 3.1 Typology for Discussion Pedagogy—Seminars

Dimensions	Seminars
Aim	1. Reach an enlarged and more developed understanding of a text 2. Improve students' levels/powers of understanding
Text	Journals, primary and secondary sources, art, music, films, ephemera
Central Question	What does the author (artist, etc.) mean?
Exemplar	Socratic seminar

Source: Adapted from the works of Walter Parker.

the field of discussion pedagogy, corroborate the challenge of teaching with and for discussion when they describe that "leading students in productive discussions of powerful texts and issues is a venerable quest in teaching" (p. 273).

There are likely several takeaways from the paragraph above. The first is that seminars have incredible potential to allow students to "plumb the world deeply" in ways that otherwise might not occur through more traditional, directive methods of instruction (Parker, 2006). The second is that the experience can create myriad permutations as it relates to students' participation and understanding related to the content. The last is that this is something so many have strived to do yet shy away from because of previous experiences. When considering discussion-based approaches, be mindful that such an undertaking can be viewed as "an incredibly difficult pedagogical feat" (Green, 1954, p. 36). While challenging in nature, it is an undertaking that needs to be explored.

It is important to begin with a few baseline understandings. First, every student in every class we teach is unique. All of them, irrespective of their skillset, have areas that need to be enhanced and supported as well as challenged. One such area that often needs support revolves around students' literacy skills. Whether using primary or secondary sources, many students struggle with literacy to the point that having them engage with meaningful texts could be potentially off-putting. Such disengagement will likely prevent them from delving into the meaningful texts and/or the ensuing seminar.

While there are countless reasons why concerns about students' literacy skills appear to be a common trend, one thing to consider is what teachers have previously been asking of them to do has, in fact, been holding them back. Recall the work by Sam Wineburg (2018) that addresses teachers' coziness with traditional approaches of reading and answering questions at the conclusion of the chapter or unit. Such approaches, while often instructionally sound, do not necessarily challenge students in meaningful ways. Thus, in some cases, it is possible that the applied instructional activities might actually be stagnating student achievement and performance.

Thus, it is important to consider how instructional approaches impact student desire and engagement. A couple of important questions should always be asked when designing lessons and instructional practices. The first question focuses on whether what you are asking of students is both rigorous and relevant. By using seminars, students are being provided opportunities to delve deeply into challenging and thought-provoking meaningful texts. Also, depending on the text(s) and centralizing question(s), students will have opportunities to tie in the content being learned with connections to their lives.

The second question focuses on whether students will perceive such activities to be meaningful and worthy of their time. By implementing seminars, students are likely to gain a sense of control and agency in their own learning. In essence, ownership of learning and productivity will be more reliant on students' efforts. In cases where students do not recognize that, it is important to share your rationale for your instructional decision-making. Aforementioned, pulling the curtain back to let students know what you are thinking can be impactful in their connection to you and the content.

By reframing our thoughts related to including seminars in our instructional practices, students are being given more opportunities to explore their deeper understandings related to the content while also improving their levels/powers of understanding. While challenging, and potentially unnerving for many teachers, students are likely to see seminars as something both challenging and unique as well as meaningful and worthy of their time.

THE DESIGN

There is no magic formula that exists as it relates to developing seminars. The absence of such a formula does not mean that there are not strategies that should be considered. Some of those considerations neatly coalesce with recent work surrounding inquiry-based approaches and the Inquiry Design Model (IDM).[1] Beginning any new task is often filled with challenges. Designing new instructional practices can create a litany of ideas that might lead to some difficult-to-escape rabbit holes. Be mindful that the process will likely have several iterations that will require a bit of patience along the way.

To begin, start with that purpose in mind. As Kohlmeier (2022) continues, seminars are intended "to engage students in a collective effort to deepen the group's understanding of a complex text" (p. 63). With that in mind, the first question that must be resolved is whether the content being chosen for the seminar presents students with a genuine intellectual tension that will lead to the development of a powerful, rigorous, and relevant centralizing question. What this means is there are some topics and content areas where using a seminar is less prudent because it might not have that tension and challenge that will drive students into deeper and more meaningful exploration.

Once there is comfort that the content is right for a seminar, the next steps will focus on either the selection of the meaningful text(s) or the development of a centralizing question. Whether you choose to begin with the selection of a text that you believe will drive students' interest or whether there is a lingering question you want to pose, the starting point is at your discretion. Irrespective of the starting point, there must be a semblance of congruence, not only between the texts selected and the question developed, but also with how and when you will implement them into your already existing practices. Again, discussion-based approaches are enhancements and should never be viewed as substitutes for already existing best practices.

In developing the centralizing question, one aim is to make sure to avoid creating a question that creates a binary or dichotomy. Students are already too hardwired to seek out the *right* answer; thus, it is important to make sure that the question presents them avenues for exploration. In order to avoid the "yes-no" and "right-wrong" questions, it might be wise to create a list, of sorts, to forecast if students are likely to develop multiple responses in their work with the text. If trouble exists in the creation of such a list, then the question might be too narrow in its scope.

It is also important to note that the question does not necessarily have to be complex or wordy. It can be simple and profound at the same time. In some cases, the less complex the question is in terms of the wording, the more students will be able to explore various meanings and interpretations. This also means that students are likely to hone in on something that you cannot forecast. Thus, it is wise to have several sub-questions ready to employ during the discussion itself. These sub-questions can serve to help students refocus and redirect the discussion itself. While seminars need to be organic and genuine in nature, concerns over addressing specific aspects of the content are still important. Creating sub-questions, or including a subsequent debriefing session, can support student understanding on topics that might not have been covered.

Developing a worthwhile centralizing question should not happen in a vacuum because it needs to have your students in mind. This means that it is important to focus students' prior knowledge and potential interests related to the content. Unsurprisingly, it is important to make sure that the question braids well with the selected text(s). Selecting meaningful texts can be a challenge and a point of contention in the design process (Apple, 1993).

The meaningful text can range in a variety of forms. It can be "a semi-permanent cultural product, such a painting, photo, script, book or letter, or an event—a transitory cultural product such as a performance or demonstration" (Cormack, 1992; as cited in Parker, 2006). The selection of such texts needs to generate interest and present a challenge—all while being appropriate for student learning. It is always important to be mindful of the biases and perspectives that are being presented.

For example, the causes of the American War of Independence are widely known and accepted. Let us say that you plan to use a question that focuses on whether or not the complaints levied by the colonists were justified. If the text presented to students only presents a colonial American perspective, then students are unlikely to even give consideration to the British perspective. As such, you might need to provide two texts to allow for students to have multiple perspectives in order to develop a more cogent and well-rounded response.

Consideration of text selection needs to move beyond just perspective. Given your understanding of your students and their needs, it is also important to create a balance in the density of the texts selected. To that end, if students are presented with a primary source that might need some scaffolding and additional support, it is suggested to use other types of texts to reduce students' cognitive load. As mentioned above, using paintings, photographs, political cartoons, maps, and charts, among other items, can support students' understandings while maintaining interest in the tasks at hand. Below are two examples (see tables 3.2 and 3.3) of seminars that I created for the study mentioned in the chapter's opening vignette. Each is provided with explanations for their creation and/or selection.

This seminar was established knowing that students often struggled with the abstract concept of nationalism and its relation to myriad changes throughout the nineteenth and twentieth centuries. In addition to the texts provided to students, students had been exposed to topics surrounding nationalism in Europe, dating back to the reign of Napoleon. The hope for this seminar—which began flatly if you recall—was to help students really explore and make meaning of the prominent "-isms" of the nineteenth century and how those "-isms" such as nationalism, liberalism, and conservatism, reached far into the events of the twentieth century. There was a particular emphasis on their relationship to World War I.

Regarding its design, the work by Phillips comes from a college-level text that provides numerous exemplars of the nationalistic fervor from several

Table 3.2 Seminar Concerning Causes of World War I: Nationalism

Meaningful Texts	Synopsis of Meaningful Texts	Central Question
Roderick Phillips (1996), *Society, State, and Nation in Twentieth-Century Europe* (pp. 51–53)	This secondary source delineates how the nationalistic fervor in the nineteenth century carried over to the early twentieth century in myriad fashions—from church sermons to lessons taught in school to popular culture of the day.	Do you believe that World War I, or another war of devastating proportions, was inevitable, given the nationalistic tendencies?
Bernhard von Bülow (1899), "Hammer or Anvil" speech	This speech by the German chancellor was given before the German Parliament, and it intended to arouse nationalistic stirrings in the burgeoning German nation.	

European nations. While a college-level text, the focus of the section students were provided had a unique relevance that was intended to pique their interest. These pages focused, in part, on how education and textbooks fed into the nationalistic frenzy. Again, the hope was that students would make relevant connections to their educational experiences as it relates to the teaching and learning of U.S. history.

The selection by Phillips was coupled with a speech by Bülow that was filled with fiery rhetoric intended to promulgate German nationalism that would match its European counterparts. The goal was for students to be able to see the relevance in the work while also being able to deepen their understanding related to the targeted objectives.

The centralizing question, while perhaps a bit too wordy, clearly identified that students' opinions on the matter were of the utmost importance. This is why it began with the phrase "Do you believe." The focus was also on the idea of inevitability. As a result of the often chronological teachings of history, most students see history as a simple cause-and-effect where the outcome is predetermined. This question also built on previous exploration related to the "inevitability" of previous events discussed in the class.

Oftentimes, when discussing topics, there is a counterpoint that could be made that an event(s) did not necessarily have to occur. In this case, students could lean on their previous engagement with such a concept. This particular seminar eventually fleshed out numerous perspectives and responses that students were able to ground in these meaningful texts.

This seminar intended to build upon students' discoveries in the seminar regarding nationalism. In between seminars, other instructional activities were utilized to support students' understandings of the content related to the causes of World War I. With this text, students were able to evaluate the correspondence of two prominent leaders of the period—Kaiser Wilhelm II

Table 3.3 Seminar Concerning Causes of World War I: Alliances

Meaningful Text	Synopsis of Meaningful Text	Central Question
Bernstein (1918), The Willy-Nicky Correspondence	This primary source, comprised of telegrams, provides students with insights into the diplomacy and negotiations that played out during the summer of 1914 between Kaiser William II of Germany and Tsar Nicholas II of Russia. These telegrams were sent in the aftermath of the assassination of Archduke Franz Ferdinand.	Do you believe that William and Nicholas genuinely sought a peaceful arrangement to ultimately prevent war, or do you believe that nationalism and militarism ultimately trumped any attempts at peace?

of Germany and Tsar Nicholas II of Russia. Both descendants of Queen Victoria, I wanted students to explore "diplomacy" in action during the summer months of 1914. It was also a way to humanize these two powerful historical figures.

The telegrams are compelling and can lead students to multiple conclusions. Again, building on prior knowledge and through their own experiential learning, students were tasked with discussing the potentials for peace coupled with the theme of inevitability. In a similar fashion to the first seminar described, it was important for students to know that their beliefs were going to be front and center. While it is not necessary to always include such phrasing (i.e., do you believe) in the question, when attempting to implement such an approach, it might be wise to include it to help students realize that you care about their beliefs. Ultimately, the goal was for students to appraise and make meaning of the materials while also being ready to defend their views.

THE DELIVERY

So many teachers consider themselves to be planners. While designing and delivering go hand-in-hand, we all know that sometimes an amazing plan does not always go accordingly. In order to support both the goals and aims of seminars and the course's requirements and timelines, it is important to consider a few steps that can keep things moving in the right direction. The list below should not be viewed as hierarchical in nature. While not hierarchical in nature, one point must be made. For seminars, and deliberations for that matter, to be successful, there will be a certain amount of modeling and scaffolding that will need to happen. The five suggestions below should provide perspective as you begin those processes.

1. **Students might be hesitant in the beginning.** It is important to remember that while the design and delivery process might be new for you, the process of learning and participation is likely also be new for them. Sometimes this hesitation stems from not wanting to look "stupid" or be "wrong" in front of their peers. Also, change can be scary, and as a result, it is important to explain the rationale for the activity in ways that are easy to understand. For many students, it quite literally might be the rarest of occasions where they are able to promote their voice. One of the most significant takeaways is to make sure not to force students to participate. Parker (2001) suggests that students be given the latitude to invite other students into the conversation. If seminars are to

occur organically, then it is important to allow students to engage when they are ready.
2. **Create a culture of active discussion and active listening.** Students are mostly offered such opportunities to participate in activities that more closely align with debates. While debates are a fine tool for exercising civic discourse, they should never be misaligned with seminars. As will be discussed in the next chapter, it needs to be shared with students that there will not be any *winners* or *losers* in the process. Seminars should be viewed as collaborative opportunities for students to learn *with* and *from* each other. Suggest to students to work on listening to, and building on, one another's comments (Parker, 2001).
3. **Be comfortable with not being the center of attention.** The focus of the exercise becomes about students interacting with each other in collaborative and meaningful ways. Of course, if there is more content that you believe needs to be addressed, it is more than appropriate to interject and add qualifying questions (i.e., sub-questions) to enhance the discussion. Additionally, by not serving as the sole gatekeeper, it is important to explain to students that they do not need to seek your approval to speak. This means that students should not be cued to have to raise their hand to speak.
4. **Provide time for thinking, writing, and reflection.** If this is a time that is intended to support students' *knowing*, then adequate time needs to be provided for rehearsal and reflection related to the text(s) and the question(s). Perhaps suggest to students to keep their ideas in their notebooks, and that their writings should be in a format that is comfortable for them. Whether they choose to write expository paragraphs or bulleted lists, the choice can be theirs. The ability for students to complete reflective writings in a manner comfortable to them will allow them to focus on the process over simply worrying about the mechanics of the product. Reframing their thinking toward the process is a game changer for students—especially those who struggle with literacy skills.
5. **Make sure to plan.** It is difficult to predict the amount of instructional planning that will be used as part of the seminars. This means that if the quality of conversation is taking longer than expected, then it will be necessary to be flexible with the remainder of the class period. The same holds true if the seminar lasts less time than expected based on previous experiences. In addition to planning as it relates to time, it is imperative to have additional instructional activities ready to use in case something in the content is not addressed.

FINAL THOUGHTS

In closing out the chapter, it is necessary to go back to the opening vignette regarding my former student who participated when no one else would. As a part of that action research study, students and their parent(s)/guardian(s) were required to sign off on their participation in the study. This simply meant that if permission was not granted, then I could not use any of that students' materials, products, recordings, or participation in the study. Fortunately, I was granted permission by all but four students.

There was also a second part that asked for permission to conduct semi-structured interviews with students if selected. Most students agreed to participate. Initially, that quiet and reserved student chose not to participate in the interview process. At the conclusion of that class, I took a minute to chat with her to see if she would reconsider. I did not want to pressure her in any way, but I wanted her to know that what I saw happen in class was something I wanted to explore. I asked her to think about it over the weekend, and it was up to her to let me know the following week.

Before class began on Monday morning, she came in early, and she asked to speak with me before other students arrived. She stated that she reconsidered and that she would be willing to be a part of such an interview. Of course, I was thrilled. Fast forward to the scheduled interviews, and as I went through the questions, I deviated slightly and plainly asked her what compelled her to participate in that very moment. Her response was simple yet powerful.

She stated that she wanted to finally be heard. Moreover, she stated that for the first time she can remember, she was actually being given the chance to be heard. In essence, she knew her beliefs and her thoughts mattered, and she wanted to take full advantage of that moment and those that would follow. What this demonstrates is the powerful potential that discussion-based approaches can have on our students. Students need to know that their ideas matter and that they have a forum by which to share them. Such a potential is important for students—not only in the moment but for their future democratic lives.

NOTE

1. It is highly recommended to read the works of John Lee, Kathy Swan, and S. G. Grant related to the Inquiry Design Model.

Chapter 4

The Deliberation

Public education and the politics of the day have been inextricably intertwined for well over a century. The change to, and ubiquity of, technology and social media outlets has allowed more people the opportunity to air their opinions and grievances to their digital friends and followers. While the sharing of ideas is just one of the many benefits of technological advancements, the back-and-forth exchange of ideas when protected by a computer screen and/ or mobile device can create "experts" out of everyone.

Whether these exchanges are focused on curricular standards or instructional materials, social studies education remains firmly pressed in the crosshairs. Given what has been shared in previous chapters, this should not be surprising. I am also wary of discussing specific political positions of the day, because as they say, if you wait long enough, there will be another issue presented in the next news cycle. Thus, the "dilemmas" of today might be of lesser concern in the years to come.

As social studies teachers, it is important to be mindful of how we ask students to engage in discussions where the goal is not so much about knowing but rather about developing ideas and making decisions related to a commonly accepted problem or issue. Discussions that are steeped in deliberative processes create moments for students to engage fully in free and open discourse that is situated as a cornerstone of our democratic republic. This, of course, will likely lead to the open exchange of ideas that are both political and controversial. While potentially intimidating, if we seek to get our students closer to the rhetoric that guides our discipline, we must challenge them and ourselves, to have these frank, candid, and respectful conversations.

Similar to seminars, utilizing deliberations is intended to enhance social studies teachers' already existing practices. An unfortunate consequence of the constrained professionalism that many of us have felt, or continue to feel, *is that our depth of knowledge related to the content and our pedagogy is routinely challenged. Discussion pedagogy should not feel like just another "flash-in-the-pan" approach that will be thrown out when a newer and shinier approach is developed and streamlined. In fact, I believe that we should work even harder to show how the work we do is paramount to the future success of our democracy.*

CONCEPTUAL OVERVIEW AND PURPOSE

Simply put, deliberations can support students even closer toward the goals and aims of social studies education. Deliberations challenge students to reframe their thinking as it relates to their role in the classroom, which can be uniquely helpful in their future lives. Just as with seminars, employing deliberations organically repositions the role of the student as a gatekeeper of information. A unique difference is that deliberations reposition students in such ways that promote a potential for their actionable decision-making. Further, deliberative discussions demonstrate moments for students to engage with a world beyond the proverbial four walls of their classrooms.

As discussed in the last chapter, seminars are intended to create a deeper sense of knowing, or enlightenment. Deliberations have a different aim. Implementing deliberations supports students in their recognition of a problem or issue of the past or in their current everyday lives. Taking it a step further, deliberations promote the political exercises associated with our democratic principles. As such, a potentially more profound aim is that deliberations push students to seek plausible and/or alternate solutions. The power of deliberations can be understood in the central question that is developed. As shown in table 4.1, it positions students to challenge themselves to consider what *they can do*.

Table 4.1 Typology for Discussion Pedagogy—Deliberations

Dimensions	*Deliberations*
Aim	1. Identify a shared problem and develop a shared solution 2. Develop a consensus/make a decision about what should be done
Text	Texts can be multifaceted but must address alternative perspectives related to the problem
Central Question	What should we do?
Exemplar	Structured academic controversy

Source: Adapted from the works of Walter Parker and Diana Hess (2001).

In addition to deliberative activities supporting students moving closer to the rhetoric and of social studies education, it also presents an opportunity to support their growth as it relates to critical thinking. As John Dewey (1916) wrote in *Democracy and Education*, "The most significant question which can be asked, accordingly, about any situation or experience proposed to induce learning is what quality of problem it solves" (p. 85). Further, Dewey contended that the presentation of problems can promote "students' natural curiosity and stimulate learning and critical thought" (Bean & Melzer, 2021, p. 2). Just the piquing of student curiosity can be challenging, but the use of deliberative exercises can facilitate interest, learning, and critical thinking—all while focused on a shared problem.

One issue often recycled from older generations to students of today is that they are blatantly unaware of contemporary issues and topics. Coupled with that derision of the current generation are the myriad *failures* of our schools and teachers. Often lost in such ridicule is that teachers and students often remain handcuffed by misguided curricular standards and expectations which, once again, lead many to become over-reliant on teacher-centered approaches. While it might feel as if this is an exercise of "screaming into the wind," it is vitally important that outside stakeholders understand this. The *feeling* that the current generation is lost and/or uninformed is a trend that seems to operate in a state of perpetuity. In fact, Wineburg (2018) suggests that such handwringing about the plight of students' civic and historical misguidedness dates back as far as World War I.

Despite the constraints that exist in social studies classrooms, you are, once again, being asked to consider how authentic approaches such as discussions can help students—now and for their future democratic lives. Diana Hess (2009), dean of the School of Education at the University of Wisconsin–Madison, proposes that schools serve as just the opportune location for discussions that support students' political engagement. She writes,

> Schools are prime sites for this type of education for three reasons. One, they have curricular opportunities for issues discussions. Two, they have teachers who are or could become skillful at teaching students how to participate, and three, in schools, there is a degree of ideological diversity that can be turned into an ideological asset. (p. 22)

By implementing meaningful discussions that are deliberative in nature, students are able to experience moments where recognition of shared problems is realized. More than simply working to gain knowledge on the topic/issue at hand, students are now afforded the opportunity to identify and address alternative perspectives in an effort to develop an acceptable, and agreed-upon, solution. This is more than just about what students "know," but rather what students "believe they can and should do."

The democratic principles of deliberations align with effective instructional methods in the social studies. Moreover, it pushes students to see the power they will hold in the future. In some ways, deliberations are akin to jury duty, as they "try to get something done when something has to be done and there is contention over the best course" (Parker, 2006, p. 13). In the end, deliberations serve as a democratically engaging opportunity that can support students' agency. Even if the topic for deliberation is limited to practices in the classroom or the school (e.g., use of cell phones, policies on grading, etc.), it situates students to plumb more deeply into prescribed materials/content while braiding their understandings related to their own agency.

Central to the purpose of deliberations remains for students "to think, speak, listen, and learn together, with and across their differences, about a specific topic" (Parker, 2006, p. 12). However, the unique part of deliberations is that learning is not the sole intended learning outcome. Deliberations serve as a form of shared inquiry that looks to evaluate a shared problem while also developing potential solutions—leading to political engagement. One way to think about the difference is seminars are used for *revealing* the world while deliberations are for *changing* the world (White, 1991). Where seminars can sometimes be misconstrued with recitation, deliberations tend to be misconstrued with debates.

An important note to distinguish is that deliberations should not be viewed as being synonymous with debates. Creating opportunities for students to engage in debates, while valuable in its own right, often connotes that opposing viewpoints will be brought forth in a competitive manner and where winners and losers will be assigned. Remember the analogy about deliberations being akin to jury duty. While juries discuss the best recourse, debates more closely align to the back-and-forth rhetoric that takes place between the defense and prosecution.

Deliberations are conceptually steeped in a collaborative ethos. While shared problems and solutions are identified and developed, it is possible for deliberations to become challenging and contentious between/among students. Given the nature of topics covered in social studies classes, coupled with the fact that so many of those topics concern various aspects of the human experience, this should not be alarming. Further, with our student populations increasing in their heterogeneity, it is imperative to give consideration to students' cultural and ethnic diversity and how their life experiences will likely shape their values, ethics, and morals.

While collaborative, students should not feel as if they must be pigeonholed into a "right-wrong" dichotomy that ultimately leads to more of a recitative exercise. In fact, students who feel pressure to acquiesce to the beliefs of their classmates and/or teacher will create, in many ways, a fatalistic result. This means that students need to believe that their voice will be heard and respected. If this does not happen, it could lead to negative feelings on multiple fronts. Students might begin to believe that neither their opinion nor the democratic process is viable.

Just the opposite is expected. Students must evaluate the shared problem from myriad perspectives while also developing a shared solution that will likely be achieved through compromise. One way to support the process is to monitor any kind of pressure-inducing language used by students during the deliberation itself. Like seminars, students need to feel comfortable sharing their thoughts. The presence of pressure-inducing language can deflate student interest in the processes associated with the deliberation, leading to student disengagement.

As shown in table 4.1, an exemplar of a deliberative approach is structured academic controversy. Given the political landscape and the contentiousness that often surrounds social studies education, the idea of promoting anything that is synonymous with academic controversy might make some wary. This is both understood and appreciated. As shared in the examples below, deliberative activities can take numerous forms and can address content that could be considered a bit less charged.

THE DESIGN

The design for implementing a deliberative method might be a bit more challenging than that of a seminar. The purpose is different, and as such, the ways in which this dialectical opportunity is framed will also likely be different. Similar to seminars, students need to be provided with a clear rationale for the exercise. In doing so, they are likely to feel a greater sense of ownership related to the task at hand. Moreover, this rationale should serve as the promotion of students as co-constructors of knowledge—not simply the passive receivers of that information which is passed on to them from the traditionally accepted gatekeepers of knowledge. Moreover, there is a distinct spirit to this type of exercise.

Helping students to understand the spirit of the exercise is, perhaps, just as important as the exercise itself (Parker, 2006). Students, in similar ways to seminars, should be reminded that actions and interactions in which they are participating should be viewed as collaborative in nature. Parker (2006) writes about this in terms of the shared ethos that can, and should, be experienced through this exercise.

The *democratic ethos* perhaps serves as the cornerstone of the deliberation in the sense that students should evaluate the problem/issue as one that is shared. As such, the potential solution should also be shared. This means, as part of democratic processing, students need to be aware of others' beliefs and thoughts. In order to fully capture the thoughts and beliefs of their classmates, they should be reminded that the process requires behaving as both active discussants and active listeners.

The *scientific ethos* is important on multiple fronts. In thinking through the topics selected for deliberation, there is much dispute that can occur. It is natural that students might rely on previously conceived notions related to a topic and will recite what has previously been learned in past classes or from those near to them, such as parents, siblings, and so on. Thus, instead of students' visceral reactions taking center stage in the development of their thoughts, students will need time and resources necessary to display and articulate informed responses. This, of course, also serves as an opportunity to share with students how they could read certain types of sources ultimately considering the potential biases that might exist. Ultimately, students will learn to become effective consumers of information and effective decision-makers.

The *collaboration ethos* is situated around the way students work together in the face of myriad possibilities that will arise during the discussion. Collaboration among students is achieved when both the democratic and scientific ethos are understood. This means that students can only collaborate in meaningful discourse when they understand the shared problem and when they take the time to evaluate sources and texts related to that problem. A lack of understanding related to those two components can quickly turn a deliberation into an uninformed debate with students seeking only to be heard and without consideration for their classmates or their thoughts.

Lastly, the *pluralism ethos* leads to an amalgamation of the previous spirits described above. In teaching about pluralism as it relates to a society or a government, the concept is based on the notion that people, governments, states, and so on, can coexist or exist on an equal plane. The perspective-taking exercise, that is a deliberation, will develop as students seek out information to support their respective beliefs in addition to evaluating alternative perspectives. This will be furthered as students serve as active listeners equally to those in agreement along with those whose ideas might differ. This democratic, co-construction of knowledge will allow for students, as a collective, to develop a plausible solution to the shared problem that originally began the exercise.

Now that the concepts, principles, and purposes are understood, where to begin? It is suggested that knowing when to "take your shot" might be as important as anything. Specifically, this means that a focus on the content and standards should guide our planning. Processes associated with the Inquiry Design Model can move the process out of the starting blocks quickly and efficiently. Thus, it is important to identify the right content angle. Finding the right content angle is a starting point that cannot be overlooked or undervalued (Swan et al., 2018). To this point, it is important to make sure that a genuine intellectual tension exists in both the standard and content being delivered. Simply put, some topics within the content do not naturally promote a deliberation. If this might be the case, then do not feel compelled to force the issue.

For a deliberation to flourish, there must also exist relevance in the lives of students that will genuinely pique their curiosity and create a natural desire to explore materials further. The first example provided below will likely create some gravitational pull from students—especially in middle and high schools. While there is neither a specific state standard nor content area identified, this topic would likely be most effective in a class focused on government or civics. In this deliberation, there exists an intellectual tension which will most likely spark visceral reactions from students, thus piquing their interest right away. In many ways, this topic should hook students almost immediately.

These texts, while not the only ones available, were vetted with several considerations in mind. First, evaluate the readability of the texts in relation to the literacy skills of your students. While this point might appear to come straight out of "Pedagogy 101," students must be able to comprehend the material being presented in addition to relating to it. Again, this is your shot to pique curiosity and promote student engagement. Thus, it is important to take every precaution to make sure the material is at grade and ability level.

Table 4.2 Deliberation Concerning Cell-Phone Policies in Schools

Meaningful Texts	Synopsis of Texts	Central Questions
NEA (2016), "By Opening the Door to Cell Phones, are Schools Also Feeding an Addiction?"	This article pre-dates the COVID-19 pandemic and addresses consequences of a more laissez-faire approach to cell-phone usage in classrooms.	Are cell phones a problem for teachers and students in classrooms? Should schools legislate student cell-phone usage in academic settings?
Lamb (2023), "Do Cell Phones Belong in School?"	This article, from the *Harvard Gazette*, presents a balanced approach that considers instructional practices, information processing, and socialization.	
PBS News Hour (2022), "Parents Pushback on Cellphones Bans at School"	This article suggests that parents should remain connected to their students due to fears of safety and being excluded from their kids' education.	

Second, assess the "density" of the material. For students in lower grade levels and secondary schools alike, it is important not to overwhelm them to the point where reading fatigue becomes apparent. Many students are used to reading on topics where character limits exist, so consider the length of the material. In this way, it is imperative to consider the "crawl, walk, run" mentality—especially in the initial attempts at this approach.

The third consideration is in some ways the most important. The texts must actually present alternate perspectives on the topic. Unknowingly, in some cases, teachers select texts that align with their beliefs and fail to provide an alternate perspective that will allow students to engage with views that differ from their own. In this particular case, teachers might have a very hardened perspective on the countless perils of cell-phone usage in academic spaces. Even so, make sure to identify texts that actually support the perspective-taken exercise.

The central questions above avoid the "right-wrong" or "yes-no" dichotomy. The first question concerning cell-phone usage as a problem is open in nature. Open, or divergent, questions such as this invite students to consider the possible perspectives that surround the topic (Saxton et al., 2018). Upon reading this question, students might develop a host of reactions given their belief that they are able to effectively multitask in class.

However, through this question and exercise, students might also begin to recognize that they might be creating an impediment to their own learning. As a result of the flow of ideas that might be immediately generated by students, asking them to connect to a question through a pre-writing activity might serve as a beneficial and reflective support for the impending discussion.

There is a potential issue with the topic, texts, and questions, being that some students might not see this as a shared problem. By embedding both teachers' and parents' perspectives in the texts and the questions, it will task them to consider others' beliefs and understandings. This is where the craft of the deliberation lies in the hands of the teacher. Being strategic in developing additional tasks along with the delivery and exposure to the meaningful texts will be an important aspect of the planning process. Of course, if amendments to the plan need to be made, be as flexible as possible to aid in the activity's success.

The second question is more heuristic (interpretive) in nature. It "guides students to discover the answers for themselves using all their resources—'knowledge, experience, imagination, and feelings' through the lens of shared problem-solving" (p. 55). Because deliberative approaches promote students to act in democratic ways, there are many possibilities that could be borne out of this experience. While students and teachers are unlikely to make wholesale changes as it relates to cell-phone policy across the school, one potential result could be the development of cell-phone policies for your classroom. As evaluated in the coming chapters, providing students' moments to make decisions about their educational experiences could present a unique opportunity to support their need for ownership.

Addressing controversy and shared problems in social studies classes is at the very heart of what should be happening. Of course, it is imperative to consider the learners and what they will need in terms of the content and the conversation. It is also important to make sure that the topics selected are not chosen to create a sense of "shock and awe" for students. Topics that surround issues related to religion, reproductive rights, or sexuality could make students feel both uncomfortable and defensive. While important to engage in challenging conversations, the ways in which the teachers approach them are paramount to their success.

The example below takes a different approach in terms of student relevancy. In some ways, it forecasts the students' role as participants in the democratic process—particularly, as it relates to voting and America's two-party system. The two-party and electoral college systems are something that can be highly charged, especially when it nears a presidential election. While students should also be paying close attention to local and state politics, nothing creates quite the buzz of a presidential election. As such, this presents opportunities to help students explore topics related to the two-party and electoral college system, as well as campaign financing and civic responsibility. The example below could be geared for classes in U.S. history, civics and economics, or government and politics.

This deliberation is actually written to work in concert with a seminar. As previously mentioned, the intersectionality of these two approaches can present students with opportunities to work toward *enlightened political engagement*. The wording of the first question was written to heighten students' curiosity. The first iteration of this question, that was later scratched, focused on the benefits and consequences of the electoral college system. Upon review, the question read in a way that students would likely feel as if they were "doing more of the same." In other words, the concern is that it would read as being too content heavy. The wording of this question can still help students address the aforementioned benefits and consequences, but it will hopefully pique their interest through the use of the possessive pronoun "your."

The second heuristic intends to promote student exploration of what other options could exist. This is where the deliberation most likely will begin. Where the first question is about "knowing," the second is more geared toward focusing on what problems exist and what other options might be viable in the United States specifically. In evaluating the possibilities, student development of a shared solution could be supported or refuted by the last article that provides students other processes utilized in other countries around the world.

Table 4.3 Deliberation Concerning the Electoral College

Meaningful Texts	Synopsis of Texts	Central Questions
National Archives (2023), "What is the Electoral College?"	This site focuses on the electoral process and the selection of the electors. It also provides information about what happens during and after the general election.	Does your vote really count in a presidential election? Should the United States maintain the electoral college or seek to develop another system?
West (2019), "It's Time to Abolish the Electoral College"	From the Brookings Institute, this article provides an abridged history of the system while also discussing why it should no longer be viewed as viable in our country today.	
The Heritage Foundation (2023), "The Benefits"	This site presents several arguments that the electoral college system preserves federalism while helping to mitigate voter fraud.	
Selsky (2020), "How do other democratic nations select leaders?"	This article, from the *Associated Press*, addresses voting practices in a case-study format, focusing on other countries' practices—to include South Africa, Poland, and Spain.	

The texts used in this example have a bit of length to them. Asking students to evaluate specific sections over others is more than appropriate. In these texts, there is a balance in perspective that is created. As always, deciding how students will work through materials created for the discussions is where the artistry of teaching comes into play.

THE DELIVERY

This book is, in no way, intended to work with universal truths or absolutes. This includes how teachers implement deliberative activities. The goal is to present the potentialities in addition to thinking through options that might present themselves. As such, the list presented below, similar to the last chapter, provides suggestions given the available scholarship and my own experiences. These "things to consider" are intended to serve as guides.

1. **Provide a rationale to students.** While some of the suggestions made might appear commonsensical, it is often the most obvious parts of the

teaching and learning process that can get overlooked. Like seminars, students need to have a shared vision of why the deliberation is taking place and how it can positively impact their learning experience. In this explanation, it might be a good idea to lean on any of the spirits mentioned above. While students might be able to see the organic nature of collaboration with seminars, this might not be as obvious with deliberations.
2. **Consider placement of the activity in your instructional planning.** Deliberations are often less predictable in the time necessary for completion. In previous experiences planning such activities, the time it takes for students to read and rehearse the texts and resources might be more time-consuming. The potential time commitment is often enhanced because students are not answering a low-level question, but rather, working through a potentially complex problem *and* trying to identify an acceptable solution. Thus, it might be wise to build the processes associated with a deliberation into multiple days within a unit. Strategically, then, you will be able to enter new information into the deliberation process which will also introduce potentially alternative positions for them to consider.
3. **Provide time for thinking, writing, and reflection.** This should look familiar from the last chapter. If teachers are suggesting to students that they are engaging in an authentic process, they must honor that process by giving the students the time to work through the posed problem. Additionally, to scaffold support of this process, it might be prudent to provide them with suggestions for how to compartmentalize their thoughts. As most of us all know, when working on a task that is new, it is easy to get stuck down any number of "rabbit holes." Help students to be more self-regulatory by guiding and monitoring their process while also providing meaningful feedback to them in real time.
4. **Help students to become more active listeners.** This suggestion serves as a segue to the next chapter. Some of the topics that will be chosen might be more charged than others. Students might need gentle reminders that this is an exercise steeped in both collaborative and pluralistic actions. Thus, with everyone on equal footing, they should work to actively listen to each other in ways that might be very different from a seminar.
5. **Help students to consider, where appropriate, how they could take action.** While the processes they are working through are, in fact, actionable, what comes after the solution might be just as important as the solution itself. The first example above regarding cell phones in schools provides such an example. When students come up with a plausible solution to the shared problem, an additional and actionable

activity might be warranted. Perhaps the next step is to identify and discuss pathways for them to take action given the solution developed. Help them to answer questions about what potential next steps would be if they wished to take it beyond the walls of the classroom.

FINAL THOUGHTS

Creating instructional activities that promote student learning and critical thinking is a large part of why we do what we do. When, as social studies teachers, we can braid that by exposing our students to democratic processes and principles, we will hit on all cylinders. Discussions, whether they be in the form of seminars, deliberations, or shared inquiries, do something else—something that could be considered even more profound. They create opportunities for us to steer our practices and students away from the transactional.

In being or remaining transactional, we continue to hold our practices, and our students' potential for achievement, hostage. This transactional approach to teaching and learning will continue in a vicious cycle of the teacher being the gatekeeper of information where students will need to memorize and recite what has been dictated to them. Moreover, it presents moments where teachers and students can move the needle against the struggle of democratic practices in classrooms (Apple, 2018). Discussions and structured discourses present a hope for a more transformative educational approach.

There is hope that with heightened awareness of practices such as discussion pedagogy, we can begin to see the possibilities that exist. Whether the potentially transformational approach be discussion-, problem-, project-, or inquiry-based is irrelevant. The more profound consideration revolves around the willingness to explore how we can support our students to be better and more active discussants and listeners; how we can facilitate their motivation; how we can build a community of learners; and how we can enhance their skills. Ultimately, we need to continue our thoughtful exploration on how we can help them be part of "The Change."

Chapter 5

The Listening

A couple of years ago, I was invited to present at a national conference where the theme focused on topics related to civic learning and democratic engagement. It was a new conference for me, and, while it was not specifically aligned with social studies education, I felt like there would be ideas and concepts I might be able to tie back into aspects of my research. On the morning I was scheduled to present, there was a session on the conference's app that I had previously overlooked. Luckily, it was scheduled before my presentation so I would be able to attend and then scurry off to find my conference room to set up my own materials.

The presenter, whose energy was palpable, drew me right in. Drawing people in during these sessions can be difficult—especially at an early hour in the morning. About five minutes into the presentation, I developed a bit of an uneasy feeling in the pit of my stomach. It was in these opening moments that I realized I might have overlooked something in my own research that should have been so obvious. That uneasy feeling quickly shifted. While I was disappointed that I might have missed something previously, I realized that this experience could help me shape this book with the addition of another chapter.

The remainder of the session was a bit of a blur for me, as I feverishly attempted to process the information being presented. I hung on every word and hoped to catch the names of every scholar mentioned. In fact, I remember feeling like I was back in some of the history courses I took during my undergrad days. The presentation was, to say the least, eye-opening. The topic that helped to cultivate my need for thinking through this chapter was based on concepts related to active listening. While active listening is mentioned in previous chapters, as it is clearly an important facet of using discussion-based approaches, I never really thought about it as a stand-alone topic. Nor did I think about how to help teachers enhance their practices to help their students' skills related to active listening.

There was one thought that I wrote down and circled on my approximately five pages of notes. That thought, which will drive a significant portion of this book, revolved around the idea that public listening is critical to the health of our democracy (Harris, 2022). This meant that if we, as social studies teachers, want to continue to close the gap between the rhetoric and reality of social studies education, helping students to engage in discussions would require another layer of consideration.

As I began my research in preparation for this chapter, I realized that I was not alone in my initial oversight—which was quite a relief. So many of the articles I identified focused on how there exists a notable deficit in terms of our understanding of the power of listening in public spaces. Additionally, it became clear that by teaching the processes associated with active listening to our students, we can, in fact, get our students closer to being more effective participants in our democratic society.

In my own experience with seminars or deliberations, I always made it a point to explain to students that the activity with which we were engaging should not be viewed as a debate. This was most likely followed up with a reminder about being respectful of their friends and classmates as well as their opinions and beliefs. It is one thing to have a "feeling" about how to promote active listening in your own practice; however, it is quite another to share that type of explanation with teachers.

Thus, here we are, adding another exciting piece to this puzzle. This extra piece is what I believe makes aspects of this book unique. My hope is that you feel the same to the point that you will consider how your practices can enhance your students' skills related to listening in public spaces. For our students to grow and develop—now and in their future lives—they need to be equipped with the ability to listen carefully and thoughtfully to others.

PRINCIPLES OF ACTIVE LISTENING

When students speak, there is much that can be discerned. Their words help us to better understand what they know and understand and their degree of preparation through our evaluation of their statements and claims. In some instances, there is a transactional nature to it. This could be part of the reason why many teachers misalign their understandings of discussion with that of recitation. Questions are raised and answers are given. From that exchange, there is much to be gleaned.

On the other hand, it is far more challenging to evaluate or assess the effectiveness with which students are actively listening to you or to each other. There is no clear-cut measurement for this. There are ways to infer by students' affect or body language or even their responses to their classmates. This can help gain some insight, but does it share everything most teachers want to know? The answer is probably not, but that is okay. With active listening, there is an internalization that students are experiencing that does not necessarily need to be understood by others.

There is a case to be made that helping students be more effective listeners is equally as important as any speaking they might do during a classroom discussion. This statement will be revisited later on in a chapter that will focus on the soft and historical thinking skills that can be developed through discussion-based approaches. Whether it be through a seminar or a deliberation, discussions are intended, in part, to create a community of learners. Whether the goal is to enhance knowledge or to work through a recognized and accepted problem, students need to understand that active listening is important for growth and progress—both their own and their classmates.

In this case, helping students to understand the importance of active listening should be viewed as transformational in nature. As mentioned in previous chapters, only when students are serving both as active *discussants* and active *listeners* can they move toward deeper levels of knowing and political engagement. As a result, they must be supported in their understanding of the power and potential of active listening as part of the larger discussion or discourse. This deeper level of understanding can push teaching and learning social studies away from recitation and memorization and closer toward how to take the knowledge gained in efforts toward taking informed action.

In conducting a search on best practices related to discussion-based approaches, much of the return focuses on what it means to support student participation as it relates to actively *speaking*. In fact, the challenge of finding credible sources related to active *speaking* is not a problem in the least. The same cannot be written for pinning down that same type of information related to active *listening* as it relates to discussion pedagogy. While these two facets of discussion-based approaches might be unequal in terms of their coverage, students' understanding related to both is, in fact, equally important.

Components related to active listening will allow for seminars and/or deliberations, or some combination thereof, to be more productive. Moreover, as students become more skilled in the ways of active listening, they will be able to share even more productive and original thoughts with their classmates. Benner (2021) shares that the definition of active listening is just that—active listening. While simplistic in definition, she continues by suggesting that active listening demonstrates a student's "genuine desire to understand the speaker's feelings and perspective without placing judgment."

While numerous definitions exist that broadly explain active listening, there are several aspects that appear to be recurrent in all of them. In unpacking the broader generalizations, work by Weger et al. (2010) breaks active listening down into three elements:

1) Active listeners' non-verbal involvement indicates that they are, in fact, giving the speaker their full attention.
2) Active listeners will reflect on comments made by the speaker while also, at times, reiterating the speaker's back to him/her.
3) Active listeners will question the speaker to promote elaboration and to provide additional details (as cited in Spataro & Bloch, 2018).

Oftentimes, the idea of listening does not seem to align neatly with being active. In fact, in modern Western culture, being silent can actually be perceived as an impediment to the conversation taking place (Spataro & Bloch, 2018). Thus, it is important to not automatically assume students are not being participatory just because they are being silent. In fact, students who are actively listening are showing respect and striving to identify and question assumptions (Ferrari, 2012; Spataro & Bloc, 2018). In many ways, for teachers, there might be some retraining that needs to be done themselves in terms of understanding the skills associated with active listening.

It might be safe to assume that everyone knows people who lack the skills associated with active listening. While talking, it might be written all over their faces that instead of intently listening to the speaker, they are merely working on what they will say next. Learning how to be a better listener, for all intents and purposes, is an important facet of healthy interpersonal relationships. This is no different from those vitally important relationships in the classroom. Thus, developing personal understandings could contribute to the support of students' skills. To be clear, being an effective listener is a skill.

It is a skill that can be developed and integrated through instructional planning, design, and implementation. But first, it is important to be able to both articulate and model those skills to students. How you choose to work this into your already packed curriculum is, of course, at your discretion. However, for discussions to be efficient, productive, and respectful, sharing ideas related to these skills with students can be just the springboard to help them be mindful of their actions and behaviors. Further, as students learn to internalize such skills, there is a greater potential for them to behave in more collegial ways.

SUPPORTING ACTIVE LISTENING SKILLS

Aforementioned, there are some limitations that exist in the literature as it relates to active listening and discussion pedagogy specifically. That being said, there are clear intersections that exist between the skills and strategies associated with active listening and discussion pedagogy. Identifying skills that are commonly associated with active listening is not the challenging part in this process. The challenge lies in the ability to teach students about the "why" as it relates to the ways in which they participate.

The need is to not only share the strategies and skills in meaningful and relevant ways, using similar instructional methods, but also to provide students with a rationale for why they should adopt these skills. Think of this in terms of scaffolding any other type of instructional activity you might implement. This type of interactive scaffolding will help students strengthen their listening skills while also helping them cultivate empathy and open-mindedness (Huynh, 2017). If students are going to buy into the process, knowing the "why" is just as important as knowing the "how."

Providing this rationale would also clearly support students' autonomy—specifically their cognitive autonomy. In supporting this type of autonomy, there is a natural inclination toward the creation of a student-centered learning environment that will encourage student initiative, in part, by using non-controlling communication. Further, students will likely feel a greater sense of ownership in the environment at large. To reiterate, the more autonomy-supportive approaches are utilized in our classrooms, the more students will benefit in terms of both achievement and motivation.

The suggestions, and corresponding explanations, that follow are intended to support a deeper level of understanding. The first such skill revolves around students effectively using **non-verbal cues** and **behaviors** that demonstrate they are actively listening. No one likes to feel as if they are not being heard. In any interpersonal relationship, people have a desire to feel that what they are saying has value and importance. While it is human nature, at times, to want to be positioned front-and-center in a conversation, effective discussions cannot occur if everyone is trying to talk without listening. Thus, students need to learn that when participating in discussions, there is an implied give-and-take that must take place.

One potential issue with helping students to signal their active, but silent, participation is the overwhelming presence of technology in classrooms today. In essence, students need to actively listen—not only with their ears—but also with their eyes and the positioning of the body. However, if students are too deeply invested in their cell phones, laptops, and/or tablets, it can give others the impression, and rightfully so, that what is being said is neither of value nor importance. For all the many splendors that technology avails, the sheer distractions technology can create can certainly thwart students' ability to genuinely engage in the discussion.

If most schools have procedures and protocols associated with cell-phone usage in class, there will most certainly be a need to reaffirm that students need to disconnect during any meaningful discussion taking place. Again, cueing students to disconnect from their technology can, at times, be an uphill battle. Thus, it will be imperative to provide students with salient reasons for this prompt.

Another suggestion for supporting students' positive non-verbal behavior focuses on the arrangement of the classroom. If possible, given the constraints of size and space, it would be beneficial to arrange the classroom in such a way that students can face each other while the discussion is taking place. It is challenging for them to show those who are speaking with their eyes that they are actively participating if they have to turn their bodies or heads in order to make eye contact. While it is easy to get comfortable with the arrangement of your room, take the time to plan how best the room can be rearranged for the discussions specifically.

One last consideration related to supporting students' non-verbal behavior includes a sort of self-regulation related to facial expressions. Statements and claims will be made that will invoke a type of visceral reaction. These types of reactions are more often based on emotion and not necessarily on intellect. Because ideas that are shared can create tension and heighten students' emotions, it will be important to monitor such behaviors and potential outbursts. This recommendation is being made for the teacher as well. We are all human, and we can react in ways that can be off-putting to students without ever saying a word. Be aware of how you react and always serve as a model for the behavior you seek from them.

A second skill is helping students to effectively **paraphrase** what their classmates are saying. This should include students learning to ask clarifying questions. For students to be able to follow up on their classmates' ideas, they should work on their ability to paraphrase what others are discussing. Additionally, paraphrasing others' ideas can help to enhance the clarity of points that are being made. A lack of understanding can lead to others' ideas being misconstrued.

When it comes to seminars, it has been suggested that students should not feel an obligation to raise their hands to participate. In the potential chaos of students trying to speak at the same time, asking students to take a pause to work on their clarifying questions can also help create a freer exchange of ideas that is presented more thoughtfully. With this skill, students will learn to build claims and statements based on those presented by their classmates. Particularly, they will begin to identify, by name, the person to whom they are responding, or on whom they are building their claim.

The use of name recognition has shown to have another potential outcome. The use of name recognition helps to enhance and build relationships in a more organic manner. There is often a belief that students know and are familiar with each other. Simply, this might just not be the case. In an action research study conducted several years ago, interviews with participating students clearly fleshed out that notion. One student stated that the seminars that were implemented in his history course helped him to get to know more about his classmates. These were classmates that he had other classes with, and he articulated how the discussions supported something as simple as learning his classmates' names (Dague, 2015).

The third skill focuses on helping students to **reserve judgment**. Again, seminars, deliberations, and structured academic controversies can present students with ideas and thoughts that run counter to the way in which they view the content. With centralizing questions and meaningful texts being written and selected with the intent of producing myriad perspectives, tensions have the potential to run high. While it is totally acceptable for students to become emotionally involved, one thing that they must learn is to hear others' thoughts to completion before deciding how to engage.

There is a well-known adage that focuses on thinking before speaking. There might not be a more appropriate colloquialism as it relates to helping students reserve their judgments. Again, if students recognize the importance of reserving judgment until the thoughts of others are more fully articulated, then they can serve as better listeners. In essence, one cannot process what is being shared when the listeners are more focused on how to respond—especially to those comments with which the listener might disagree.

The same inclination to verbally pounce on classmates with whom they disagree—without fully listening and understanding—can kill the learning climate quicker than just about anything else. Reminding students before each discussion that taking the time to pause before responding can do two things. The first is that it allows others to fully develop their thoughts without interruption. The second is that the pause can help students collect their thoughts while also being more mindful of their tone and tenor. Disagreements are likely going to happen. That is both expected and accepted. However, the ways in which students disagree need to be addressed whenever necessary.

The fourth, and final, skill that students need to develop aligns neatly with the last. Students can become more proficient active listeners as they learn to be more **reflective**. Again, the goal of promoting active listening is not to apply an alphanumeric grade related to students' performances. In fact, it could be argued that the discussion itself should never be graded. This should be reiterated to students that participation is something that they should want to do. As such, the teacher's role should serve as that of a facilitator.

Through this facilitation, there might be moments where you will need to intervene to stoke the discussion or to quell students talking over each other. The reflective portion of active listening could include you periodically intervening to ask students to reflectively write what they have heard up to that point or even throughout the discussion that has taken place. Through written reflection, students will be able to gain granted time to rehearse and reflect on what they have heard, what they know, and how they might participate in the remainder of the discussion.

INFORMATION PROCESSING AND ACTIVE LISTENING

Building on the fourth skill mentioned earlier, providing students with opportunities to be reflective can not only improve students' active listening, but it can also enhance the ways in which they process information. While discussions can take many shapes, providing moments for reflection can give students the opportunity to effectively listen while also helping them to manipulate and strategize about the information that they have taken in (Santrock, 2020).

Several models exist that detail the processes associated with information processing. The figure presented below (Figure 5.1) is referred to as the Multi-Store of Memory Model. Developed by Atkinson and Shiffrin (1968), this presents a simplified depiction of how students take in information through their sensory registers all the way to storing it in their long-term memory.

This opportunity for rehearsal and reflection can also support students' ability to process information more effectively for later use. As students are taking in information through their senses, they must parse what information to keep and what they should push off to the side. As pertinent information is processed and reaches the short-term/working space in the memory, there is a need for opportunities to rehearse and continue their work with the information. This could take shape in the form of auditory and/or rehearsal

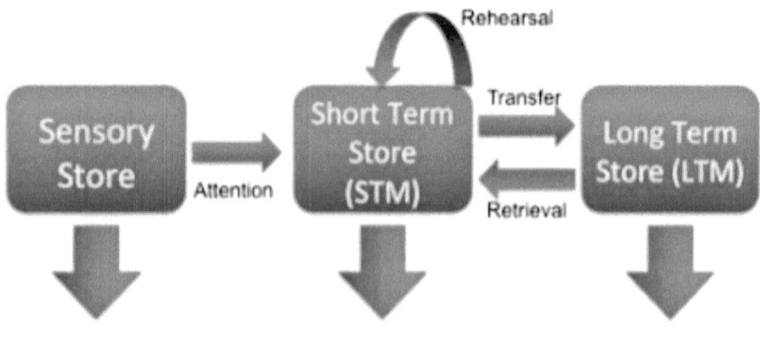

Figure 5.1 Multi-Store of Memory Model

practices. When students are given the time, regardless of the reason, it will allow them to better encode the information and transfer it into their long-term memory. This could lead to a greater likelihood of being retrieved in the days to come. Thus, supporting those moments can have many benefits for students.

Shown as a sort of recursive cycle are opportunities for auditory and visual rehearsal. This rehearsal, as it relates to active listening and discussion-based approaches, can take on many forms. What is known is that the more effectively students use their working memory, the more effectively they will be able to regulate their learning and memory. This is all written to suggest that while the discussions need to include student ownership, there are opportunities to facilitate the pace and the in-discussion activities that could support both active listening and the rehearsal strategies for processing the information being taken in.

Additionally, moments for rehearsal can help to refocus students' attention. As students take in and process the information being shared with them by their classmates, concepts and ideas that students identify as being both meaningful and viable help to maintain their attention. If attention is deviated or lost for whatever reason, information can also be lost in the process. Assuming that students' attentions are maintained by the discussions occurring, what becomes important about information-processing models is what will happen in the short-term, or working, memory.

Thus, if there is a perceived need for students to take time to reflect on what they have heard, it would be wise to have a few assessment techniques prepared for students to work through. Classroom Assessment Techniques, developed by Angelo and Cross (1993), provide suggestions in which students could demonstrate their active listening through succinct, formative assessments. Again, this is not an exercise in evaluating for a grade but rather to help braid the active listening necessary for the discussion and the rehearsal for the information being processed.

Students could be asked to work through a brief "minute paper" or a "directed paraphrasing" assignment where they would paraphrase part of the discussion into an easy-to-understand vernacular. You could even ask students to use a common instructional strategy like Think-Pair-Share. Regardless of the instructional method utilized, time for rehearsal should be integrated appropriately to support both the discussion and student learning.

FINAL THOUGHTS

Helping students learn the skills associated with active learning might be just as challenging as encouraging them to actively participate through speaking.

For one, students who sit quietly are often thought to be apathetic or aloof. As such, they might feel compelled to speak in moments where they have not meaningfully processed what has already been shared by others. This can certainly occur when teachers use discussions as an opportunity for forced engagement and participation. While there are opportunities for students to be evaluated based on the discussion, grading them on the number of times they actively speak is counterproductive to the organic nature of discussions. Moreover, it pushes students to, going back to the previously mentioned adage, speak before they listen.

Secondly, it is challenging to teach students how to keep hold of their emotions and ideas during a discussion. Much of the interaction seen in public spaces or on social media is filled with people reacting without truly processing what others have said or written. While all too commonplace, students must focus on reserving their judgment until they are able to fully process what their classmates have shared. Through paraphrasing or asking clarifying questions, students will have to process first in order to respond more effectively. None of this can be done without actively listening.

Finally, teaching students the skills of how to effectively speak to each other can appear to be much more of a simple task because the words that they use indicate their degree of understanding and their ability to show respect to each other verbally. However, finding time and space in an already constrained schedule to scaffold support for active listening might appear to be a fool's errand. However, the connections between supporting these active listening skills and discussion pedagogy are, in fact, paramount to the success of the discussion itself. With this type of scaffolding, there will be a bit of trial-and-error involved.

These moments can involve using Classroom Assessment Techniques too early or not early enough. It could also include not being able to get students to totally detach from their cell phones or provided instructional technology. These moments could also result in you being unable to truly relinquish a significant portion of the control that you are used to. All of these moments are common, but with that being said, they need to be addressed and amended so that students can get to the desired end state—whether it is to share their knowledge or to dialectically work through a problem. It takes work and effort—from both your students and you.

Chapter 6

The Motivation

In my thirteen years in the classroom, I was fortunate to work in a diverse school that was full of dedicated administrators, faculty, and staff. I was in a place where the development and growth of students stood front and center. I respected my colleagues in the social studies department, in part, because of their unique and thoughtful instructional design. I also admired the meaningful relationships they developed with their students.

Perhaps most importantly, in each of these teachers, I observed an unmistakable passion for their content and students alike. Yet even the best of these teachers experienced moments of struggle—most notably when it came to motivating students. How could this be? These teachers cared so much for their students and the content they were teaching, and yet, there were these notable moments of struggle to motivate and engage their students.

Finding answers to the question of how best to motivate students has been central to my work over the past decade. As both a teacher and a coach, I have been fascinated to learn more about the factors that drive my students and my players. I have questioned how and why the experiences I created motivate them to perform in the classroom and/or on the field. I have questioned how my methods influence them and their efforts.

This fascination became grounded early in my doctoral program as I became immersed in both seminal and burgeoning theories and concepts related to motivation and its influence on learning and achievement. These experiences gave me pause to think about and reflect, on my influence on student motivation in my classroom. As I learned new theories and concepts, I routinely brought them back to my classroom and utilized them strategically to evaluate if any impacts were apparent.

Then, I came across what I believed to be the holy grail of conceptual frameworks. One of my committee members introduced me to self-determination theory (SDT) as a potential framework for the action research study that would lead to my dissertation. It would also set the table for future research projects and scholarship opportunities. To this day, my belief in its principles continues to grow. Application of SDT in my social studies classes ranged from the ways in which I interacted with students (e.g., controlling motivating vs. autonomy supportive) to amendments I made in my instructional delivery.

Such changes included a conscious shift from the directive practices with which I was most comfortable toward approaches that were more discussion-, project-, and/or inquiry-based. The changes were difficult as it required a stemming of the tide of the historical storytelling that I so enjoyed. While the repositioning of the classroom became a focal point for implementation, which also gave me some trepidation, the benefits of the shift became clear and evident. Thus, my interests accelerated in ways I could never have imagined.

A NEED FOR EXPLORATION

The time to design and deliver authentic learning experiences in social studies classrooms is now. Today, so much of a teacher's focus is predicated on standardized testing and evaluating student *performance*. Understanding measurable outcomes related to formative and summative assessments is an important aspect of the teaching and learning process, but it should not be the only aspect of the process. In fact, the impact of over-relying on standardized tests as the sole measure for student and school success continues to be scrutinized. The late Elliott Eisner (2001), champion for arts education, posited that the "formulation of standards and the measurement of performance were intended to tidy up a messy system and to make teachers and administrators truly accountable" (p. 367).

Failed reform efforts and political jockeying have led teachers and students to experience immense pressure to perform on high-stakes tests. Expected student performance on standardized tests has routinely led teachers to be treated as something more akin to that of dutiful technicians in the classroom (Giroux, 1985). This often results in a superficial "covering" of the prescribed curriculum through stand-and-deliver methods that prevent students from experiencing deeper and more meaningful learning opportunities. In what should not be a surprise, such an overreliance on stand-and-deliver, teacher-centered methods leave many students listless and apathetic to the learning process entirely.

The seemingly routine curricular revisions made by each of the fifty departments of education provide cause to evaluate the curricular tensions that exist in our courses. As teachers, the ability to change the prescribed curriculum is limited. One of the foci of this book is to consider how authentic instructional approaches, such as discussion pedagogy, can motivate, energize, and grow our students—all while meeting the prescribed curriculum. These kinds of efforts can lead toward the building of a new kind of social studies classroom that promotes both student *enlightenment* and *political engagement*.

This chapter serves as a conduit of sorts. While keeping the strategies and benefits of discussion pedagogy front of mind, there is a need to unpack, in a more robust manner, several facets and considerations related to motivation for teaching and learning. Emphasis will be given to (1) defining motivation, (2) differentiating between *intrinsic* and *extrinsic* motivation, (3) reviewing perspectives on motivation, and (4) outlining the framework for SDT as a conceptual framework that can help us rethink motivation in our classrooms. Ultimately, this chapter will set the table for how discussion-based approaches can support and promote students' motivation and psychological needs moving forward.

CONTEXTUALIZING AND DEFINING MOTIVATION

Identifying and utilizing strategies that motivate students in our classrooms is challenging and complex. It is important to begin by thinking about motivation for learning and achievement in bidirectional and reciprocal terms. To that end, there is a need to recognize how the strategies and practices that teachers employ, along with the overall learning climate created, influence students' motivation. As students are expected to be responsible for their actions, we must also hold ourselves to the same standard. This is an important point because, as teachers, we are susceptible to placing blame on the shoulders of students when they appear uninterested and disengaged.

In fact, it is not uncommon to hear colleagues remark on how students of today are very different from those in years' past. While there might be contextual differences that make each generation unique and challenging, rest assured that commonalities do, in fact, exist. When thinking in terms of motivation, consideration should be given to students' abilities while also factoring in how cultural and ethnic backgrounds influence their behaviors. Given just these two facets, it is easy to see how pinpointing what drives our students seems to be a bit of a moving target—not just year-to-year—but day-to-day!

Reviewing two definitions on motivation seems like a prudent place to begin. John Santrock (2020), a noted developmental psychologist, defines motivation as the "processes that energize, direct, and sustain behavior" (p. 430). Others in the field of motivational psychology suggest that motivation is the "process whereby goal-directed activity is instigated and sustained"

(Schunk et al., 2008, p. 4). Subtle differences exist in the definitions; however, two aspects appear to overlap. The first is that motivation is a *process* rather than a *product*. The second is that the processes related to motivation require *sustained* activity.

The focus on process is important when situated against the backdrop of various educational reform efforts. The emphasis placed on the results of standardized tests calls into question whether the pressures to pass these tests increase students' motivation to learn or lead many to "give up in the face of failure" (Alderman, 1999, p. 8). Moreover, there is a need to be attentive to how standardized tests influence expectations either placed on or internalized by students. This is important because teachers' expectations of their students' performance lead them to approach teaching in ways that align with those expectations.

Additionally, reconsidering the point about the bidirectional/reciprocal nature of motivation, if a teacher has low expectations, then students tend to perform at those low levels (Lynch, 2016). Moreover, there is a need to examine if our instructional practices are simply teaching to the test. If so, then it is likely that we are missing out on supporting and promoting students' motivation—especially those who might give up because of failure.

Going back to Santrock's (2020) definition, *energy* can serve as a springboard for directing action when working toward a goal or task. To make the point clearer, let us think about an example related to our energy as teachers. After reading the first few chapters in this book, you might begin to contemplate ways in which you can integrate discussion-based approaches in your class. Believing there are benefits, there is hopefully a heightened sense of excitement as you think through identifying meaningful texts and developing centralizing questions. Additionally, you might even begin to imagine how your students will positively react and engage with this new addition to your instructional toolbox. As a result, your energy and action are moving you toward making this instructional amendment and will likely direct you toward subsequent actions.

Your process might begin by searching for meaningful texts on an upcoming lesson. You find that locating that perfectly enticing text is proving more difficult than expected, or perhaps you find a text you like, but you believe that it might not be appropriate for any number of reasons. As a result, frustration begins to creep in as you hit a few roadblocks. In reaching this proverbial fork in the road, you will need to make decisions about how, or if, you will continue to work toward the goal that excited and energized you at the beginning.

One option includes developing a plan for seeking the meaningful text while also refining some of the language for easier processing, if necessary. Another option is to delay or give up on your pursuit of the instructional amendment. As a teacher, you have undoubtedly encountered these kinds of roadblocks. What you learned from similar experiences will likely help your next steps. If you are a pre-service teaching candidate reading this section, these types of issues arise frequently. Regardless of teaching experience, you will need to *direct* your attention toward the importance of seeing the goal through to completion.

Simply put, when facing obstacles, the condition of "fight or flight" usually becomes evident. Energy and the direction of actions taken, or not taken, is a response to the difficulties, problems, and setbacks encountered. The ability to reconcile and navigate these types of events will direct and *sustain* your subsequent behavior and actions. Directing and sustaining your behaviors and actions can be a struggle, causing your motivation to wax or wane.

Looking at motivation as part of a teacher's professional practice is notably different from the motivation related to students. When considering student motivation, the definition does not change; however, the frame of reference does. One significant difference from the example above is that students might not have the tools related to concentration, persistence, volition, and strategies for acquiring and retaining new information to be successful. Many students do not have the life experience or wherewithal from which to build. This is what makes a teachers' role in student motivation so vital. Beyond simply teaching the content, it is necessary to support and guide students as they begin and direct their actions toward a goal. One problem is that many teachers have not acquired the instructional strategies necessary to foster positive motivation (Alderman, 1999). When thinking through those instructional strategies, keep three questions in mind:

1. How will the actions we take *energize* or *activate* our students' behavior?
2. How can we support and *direct* our students' behavior?
3. How can we guide students to be *persistent* or *sustaining* in their behavior?

Particular attention to question two is paramount to student learning and achievement. Many students are not equipped to identify and utilize self-regulatory behaviors to be persistent in their actions. Self-regulation includes the process where students can activate and sustain behaviors in systematic ways toward the achievement of a task or goal. Due, in part, to students' prior experiences, we need to understand what influences students' motivation and how it differs and manifests itself whether we are working with young children or teenagers. Such an understanding of what drives students and how they handle the challenges and adversity they will face will help support their persistence toward a goal or task. It is important to pay close attention to students' belief related to their self-worth and their ability as it plays a key role in directing and redirecting their behaviors.

INTERPLAY OF INTRINSIC AND EXTRINSIC MOTIVATION

Building on the definitions above, it is important to differentiate between *intrinsic* and *extrinsic* motivation. Intrinsic motivation refers to the motivation to engage in an activity for the sake of the activity itself. Students, much like adults, are more willing to participate and actively engage when a goal or task is enjoyable. As such, participation in an activity is its own reward and does not depend on external rewards or other constraints (Schunk et al., 2008). With this understanding in mind, the goal should always be to deliver tasks and assignments to which each of our students gravitates. While that should still be a goal, the likelihood of delivering on that goal is improbable. As such, it is necessary to also consider the role that extrinsic motivation plays in the teaching and learning process. Extrinsic motivation is motivation deemed to serve as a means to an end. Further, it directs people to "work on tasks because they believe that participation will result in desirable outcomes such as a reward, teacher praise, or avoidance of punishment" (Santrock, 2020, p. 236).

Both intrinsic and extrinsic motivations are contextually sensitive, meaning that they characterize people at a given point in a given activity. This means that some students will experience and display varying degrees of both intrinsic and extrinsic motivation in a class and in relation to activities and tasks. Helping to facilitate our students' intrinsic motivation should remain the goal. While that might be challenging, Harter and Connell (1984) posit that five assumptions can be made regarding students and their intrinsic motivation. Their research suggests that students prefer

- challenging rather than easy work;
- satisfying their own interests and curiosity rather than working to please the teacher to earn a grade;
- independent attempts at mastery with less dependence on the teacher;
- independent judgment rather than reliance on the teacher's judgment; and
- internal criteria for success and failure rather than external criteria.

There is also research to support that students' intrinsic motivation appears to lessen as they get older (Harter, 1981b). This might be a result of schools "gradually stifling children's intrinsic interest in learning, specifically with regard to challenge, curiosity, and independent mastery" (pp. 309–310).

Many early childhood learners demonstrate higher degrees of intrinsic motivation because of encouragement from teachers and parents to "figure out how things work, discover their own capabilities and limitations, and master various problems" (Ryan & Deci, 2018, p. 352). Additionally, the lessening of intrinsic motivation could be a result of an increase in the use of external controls, such as grades and standardized test scores.

In thinking about the preferences listed above, the common thread throughout is that students want more control, or autonomy, in their educational experiences. Thus, it is reasonable to suggest that educational settings could support improving students' intrinsic motivation by increasing the "challenge, interest, and relevance of the curriculum" while "minimizing reward systems" that appear to be common practice (Lepper et al., 2005, p. 185). Moreover, students who demonstrate higher degrees of intrinsic motivation tend to have greater self-esteem along with an overall well-being. Given what is known, facilitating students' intrinsic motivation needs to be a focal point in the development of our instructional practices. Of the three perspectives discussed below, two of the three lean on that very suggestion.

MOTIVATIONAL PERSPECTIVES

In an effort toward further unpacking student motivation, reviewing various perspectives is the prudent next step. The three perspectives below can be learned discretely; however, it will become clear that synergies and intersections exist between and among them. To build toward deeper understandings related to motivation, it is necessary to evaluate and reflect upon each perspective. Each of these perspectives demonstrates value, but depending on your beliefs and experiences, certain aspects might be more meaningful.

Behavioral Perspective

Behaviorist principles and theories might lead to memories of learning about Ivan Pavlov and his salivating dogs (classical conditioning) or even B. F. Skinner and his theories related to the use of reinforcements (operant conditioning). Both theories are important to the field of learning and can be helpful to our understanding of motivation. Similarly, behavioral perspectives focus on the use of external rewards and/or punishments as determinants in a student's motivation. A behavioristic perspective situates motivation "by the rate or likelihood of behavior" (Schunk et al., 2008, p. 20). Thus, the use of incentives in the classroom—in either positive or negative manners—can serve to motivate a student's behavior.

Incentives commonly serve as a frontline approach to motivating students. The use of grades, gold stars, certificates, or other rewards/reinforcements might promote the types of actions and behaviors necessary to direct students' actions toward a goal or task. This could also include the removal of something undesirable if students' actions align with behavior deemed appropriate.

In contrast, over-relying on external rewards and incentives has a few consequences. The first reflects on the adage that a human's wants are insatiable and that they will never be satisfied with what they already have. For example, for a highly motivated student who excels in class, an alphanumeric grade will only hold their motivation for a period of time. Thus, if there are no changes to incentives or rewards, the student's motivation might diminish on future goals and tasks. In this case, if seeking to facilitate the student's motivation, teachers should lean more on challenging and meaningful approaches through differentiated instruction. A second consequence is that the behavioral perspective, as an explanation for motivation, does not factor in a student's thoughts and feelings because the belief is that they are motivated by environmental factors (Schunk et al., 2008, p. 20). As will be discussed later, this perspective also minimizes the role of intrinsic motivation toward learning and achievement.

Cognitive Perspective

The cognitive perspective takes a more internal approach to motivation in that it stresses additional factors, such as "perceptions of competence, values, affects, goals, and social comparisons" (Schunk et al., 2008, p. 21). While behavioral perspectives focus predominantly on the external, cognitive approaches address and acknowledge the role of intrinsic motivators. In essence, a student's thoughts and feelings are important in guiding his or her motivation. This internalization can support students to enhance their motivation toward mastery. Additionally, the cognitive perspective creates a shift of sorts related to application in the classroom. With more of a focus on responsibility and control of achievement outcomes, students can become more active in their educational process.

By providing additional autonomy, students can take action *within* their environment and not necessarily *because* of their environment. While this might appear to be a superficial distinction, it speaks to larger motivational concepts. Such an increase in responsibility provides students with opportunities to evaluate and reflect on facets related to their direction and self-regulation. This could include students

- reflecting on their confidence-related task performance;
- analyzing what they perceive to be successful and unsuccessful performances;

- judging their own performances; and
- deciding if/how they will attempt, complete, and/or repeat activities (Bruning et al., 2011, p. 7).

Supporting students' awareness related to their self-regulation can have lasting impacts on their motivation when approaching more challenging goals and tasks in the future. Self-regulated learners have

- adaptive attributional beliefs, accepting responsibility for their learning;
- a strong sense of self-efficacy;
- a belief that effort will lead to increased success; and
- tools for setting effective goals (Alderman, 1999).

Social Perspective

Social perspectives on motivation, as likely expected, focus primarily on relationships and feelings of belongingness. The need for affiliation or relatedness emphasizes a need to create and maintain secure relationships with others. Briefly mentioned earlier in the chapter, the social perspective is steeped in the need to consider how a teacher's actions and behaviors as well as demeanor impact student motivation. In essence, students are more likely to be motivated when they are a part of a warm and welcoming learning environment.

A student's need for affiliation is reflected in their motivation to spend time with peers and friends along with the positive relationships they build with their teachers. Research on the importance of teacher-student relationships is consistent in that "when teachers respond to students in ways that are responsive to student needs, are emotionally warm, and provide for student autonomy, students tend not only to feel more motivated in the classroom, but also achieve at higher rates" (Davis & Dague, 2020, p. 153).

The social perspective demonstrates meaningful intersectionality with other theories and principles. As students feel enhanced degrees of belonging to a classroom and/or school setting, improvements in motivation, social-emotional well-being, engagement, and academic functioning are positively impacted. There is also research to suggest that warm, welcoming, and autonomy-supportive relationships serve as a deterrent to student absenteeism and dropout rates (Korpershoek et al., 2020).

SELF-DETERMINATION THEORY

SDT was pitched earlier as being a theoretical holy grail of sorts. There are several reasons for what might appear to be a bold proclamation. First, it recognizes and honors the importance of the three perspectives described above—to include the influence that both intrinsic and extrinsic motivation plays in students' learning and achievement. Second, it encourages student engagement and agency in their own educational process. Third, it promotes the need to rethink classroom environments through the use of autonomy-supportive motivating styles.

SDT is a macro-theory that focuses on the factors and conditions that support or impede a person's assimilative and growth-oriented processes (Niemec & Ryan, 2009). As its cornerstone, it posits that people are naturally curious and willing to explore their worlds—especially when the conditions are ripe and fulfilling. A person's intrinsic motivation can be facilitated when circumstances permit. Such conditions and circumstances require a person to be able to exercise control over their environment in order to satisfy their respective needs. In other words, students need opportunities to behave in self-determining ways.

It might be a bit of a broken record at this point, but there is an imperative to evaluate how schools and classrooms consider students' needs—especially as it relates to their intrinsic motivation. Such overreliance on external controls and extrinsic motivators (e.g., grades, rewards, etc.) often thwarts students' intrinsic motivation toward meaningful learning and creativity. Again, this is not to blame teachers for their unwillingness to grow and adapt in this area. As previously mentioned, "many modern schools have become extremely focused on a *very* narrow set of cognitive goals, often to the neglect of the varied interests, talents, and more holistic psychological and intellectual needs of students" (Ryan & Deci, 2018, p. 353). As such, external controls that align with behavioral perspectives on motivation often take precedence in order to reach identified performance goals.

Richard Ryan and Edward Deci conceptualized SDT in the early 1980s, proposing that all students are innately motivated intrinsically; their lack of perceived control and power, as well as agency over their learning environments and experiences, reduces their potential for commitment and responsibility. Earlier research by deCharms (1976) described a binary in terms of the perceived roles that students play in most classrooms. He referred to students as either "Origins" or "Pawns." Origins are students who are able to act in autonomous ways, whereas Pawns act as powerless participants. Similarly, Freire's (2014) "banking model" of learning assumes that many of our students see themselves as Pawns.

The negative implications are clear when students perceive a lack of control over their learning. First, students who feel powerless are more likely to demonstrate tendencies of apathy and passivity. Conversely, students who perceive their surroundings to be more Origin-like "reported greater internal control over outcomes and higher perceived competence and mastery motivation" (Schunk et al., 2008, p. 250). All of this is to say that when students feel a sense of control, they are more likely to seek to master a task or goal because they have a greater likelihood to believe in themselves and their ability. The second consequence is that students have a more difficult time dealing with adversity in their environment—which will likely undermine their intrinsic motivation (Glass & Singer, 1972). Ultimately, this might result in students losing interest in their environments, leading to a decrease in engagement.

Based on our understanding of motivation and SDT, there are several considerations that can be applied to our classrooms. SDT stipulates that students are innately curious and have a natural love for learning. As such, there is a need to find ways to cultivate that desire while also facilitating their intrinsic motivation. While recognizing that both intrinsic and extrinsic motivation are important in student learning and achievement, countless reasons have led many of us to rely too heavily on external controls to motivate our students. SDT refers to these two camps as autonomy-supportive and controlling-motivating styles. Table 6.1 provides a breakdown of each—to include instructional behaviors associated with each.

FINAL THOUGHTS

While the next chapter will plumb more deeply into the importance of shifting to autonomy-supportive motivating styles, it is valuable to leave you with a singular point. As Ryan and Deci (2000) wrote very simply, "Motivation

Table 6.1 Characteristics of Autonomy-Supportive and Controlling-Motivating Styles

Controlling-Motivating	*Autonomy-Supportive*
Definition Interpersonal and instructional behaviors that pressure students to think, feel, and behave in a specific way.	Definition Interpersonal and instructional behaviors that identify, nurture, and develop students' inner motivational resources.
Instructional Behaviors: • Direct instruction as the primary method of instruction • Limited student choice • Focus on performance goals • Utilize pressure-inducing language • Display impatience to produce the right answer • Assert power in response to students' complaints and/or negative affect	Instructional Behaviors: • Authentic instructional methods utilized • Choice provided in the form of assessments • Focus on achievement goals • Reliant on non-controlling language • Display patience to allow for self-paced learning • Accept expressions of concern and negative affect

Source: Adapted from the works of Johnmarshall Reeve.

produces." Now the task becomes to pinpoint how to best support your students' needs. Perhaps more importantly to the focus of this book, there is a need to explore how discussion-based approaches in your social studies classes can do just that.

The intersections that exist between discussion-based approaches and facilitating students' motivation show clear correlations. They create opportunities for teachers to balance needs related to both intrinsic and extrinsic motivation. Discussions present students with choices while also creating learning experiences that can match and challenge their individual and collective skills. Also, and in real time, discussions can be rewarding for students because of the feedback they will receive from you and their classmates alike.

In addition to thinking about the various perspectives and theories presented earlier, there is a potential that meaningful discussions could also enhance participants' self-efficacy. In this case, these enhancements are not just solely beneficial to students. Of course, as students grow in their beliefs related to their abilities, they will also begin to seek out additional challenges and be more eager and willing to persevere in the academic tests they will face.

That being said, a teacher's enhanced self-efficacy will assuredly have a major impact on the quality of learning that students experience. While many authentic instructional methods exist for social studies teachers, discussions can serve as a gateway to help build and support teachers' confidence and self-efficacy. As students' growth and development improves through these techniques, it will provide moments for your own pedagogical growth. As such, it will open doors for you to implement other such meaningful approaches. Thus, the motivation and confidence that you feel and exude will undoubtedly make the right impression on your students while launching the trajectory of your classroom.

Chapter 7

The Support

In thinking about the countless ways that teachers provide support to their students, I am reminded of a piece written by Elliot Eisner and Larry Cuban in 2013. Aptly titled "On Teaching," Eisner and Cuban outline what they identify as the six satisfactions of teaching. It is a short article used routinely in my methods courses with both pre- and in-service students. Often shared early in the semester, it provides my students with a much-needed reminder of the enormity of how a teacher's support can positively promote student growth and development.

From the beginning, the article is situated to suggest that too many policymakers have never taught in public schools, and as such, they struggle to recognize "what it is about teaching young children, youth, and adults that binds teachers and students together." After unpacking each of the six satisfactions, Eisner and Cuban make it a point to elucidate that the satisfactions of teaching extend well beyond the academic. They suggest that the "most lasting contributions come from rescuing a child from despair, restoring a sense of hope, [and] soothing a discomfort." This serves as a reminder that part of our professional imperative is to "remember that the student is a whole person who has an emotional and social life, not just an intellectual one."

In addition to the social-emotional support often positioned in the front of our minds, there are other supports that must be explored in order to promote the psychological needs of students. Supporting and promoting these needs can have just as much influence on students—now and in their future lives. These three needs became apparent to me while I was drafting one of countless iterations for my first action research project. Having already identified self-determination theory (SDT) as my conceptual framework, I wanted to know how an authentic intervention—discussion pedagogy—would impact student engagement and motivation. Thumbing through articles and available scholarship, I continued to think about the role and support of these three needs.

The three needs to which I am referring are autonomy, competence, and relatedness. These needs became a focal point for me. As I would do more digging, I would make subtle amendments to my own instructional practices to see what the outcomes would be. What I observed gave me the confidence to continue forward with that action research project and others since.

As I saw it, my AP social studies courses were designed to do two things. The first was to challenge my students to think critically and historically. The second, with most of my students heading off to a four-year institution, was to prepare them with the skills required to navigate the classes they would take in their post-secondary lives, which included handling classes that were steeped in direct instruction. While confident that my classes were both challenging and preparatory, I became keenly aware that I was only scratching the surface of what they really needed.

My students needed ownership of, and agency in, their learning. They needed choice in their learning experiences and how they would be evaluated. They needed to have a voice, and they needed to be able to use this voice to engage and interact with their classmates in more organic and meaningful ways. This eventually led to the questions that have guided my research ever since, which revolve around how systematic implementation of discussion pedagogy promotes and supports student autonomy.

UNDERSTANDING STUDENTS' NEEDS

Attempting to understand all that students need is just one facet of being an effective teacher. Schools have become increasingly diverse with class sizes that are, on average, larger than in years' past. Identifying strategies to support students' needs, through the lens of SDT should not feel like another layer of responsibility for teachers. In fact, many teachers likely have existing practices that already align with SDT principles.

In order to promote students' psychological wellness and intrinsic motivation, it is important to enhance our understanding related to these principles and how they can be embedded. Previous chapters elucidated the power and potential of discussion pedagogy through delivery of seminars and deliberations. Now, the focus is to display how discussion pedagogy can serve as a conduit for supporting students.

Supporting students' basic innate psychological needs creates a unique intersection and coalescence with the much-needed social-emotional support described above by Eisner and Cuban. Such support can be leveraged in ways to help build on the power and influence of the teacher-student relationship.

Often, the needs for satisfaction of students' autonomy, competence, and relatedness are supported through instructional design and delivery. That is the focus here. However, in no way is that intended to diminish the importance of the interpersonal bonds developed and maintained between teachers and students.

Supporting the whole child is hard. Identifying and making the *right* decision is typically based on previous professional and educational experiences. There is no tried-and-true exactness in supporting students, especially given their diversity and unique needs. Thus, the most prudent place to begin is by unpacking the nuances of autonomy support and the corresponding strategies since the available research suggests that supporting students' autonomy serves as a springboard for also supporting their competence and relatedness.

In terms of motivational processes, autonomy refers to one's need to feel a sense of control and agency in their environment. As teachers, there exists a need to feel a sense of ownership in the decisions made in our classroom. Believe it or not, students feel the same need. Students will feel enhanced degrees of autonomy when they are engaged in activities and behaviors that allow them to exert their will, or volition, in the learning environment.

For some teachers, providing students with choices and agency might appear to be a slippery slope. Some teachers might rely on the adage that if you give students an inch, then they will take a mile. As such, the thought of implementing strategies where students are provided with some semblance of ownership can create trepidation for teachers. This is not at all uncommon.

In fact, teachers' fear of giving up the proverbial reigns is one of the many reasons that they traditionally stick to what is referred to as controlling-motivating or authoritarian strategies. As Reeve and Halusic (2009) enumerate in an article titled, "How K-12 Teachers Can Put Self-Determination Theory Principles into Practice," teachers often have very similar questions when thinking through applying autonomy-supportive strategies. Some of these questions include the following:

- What is the goal of autonomy-supportive teaching?
- Does autonomy support mean permissiveness?
- How would I encourage students' initial engagement in learning activities?
- What would I say? How might I talk?
- How do I know if I provided instruction in an autonomy-supportive way?

The desire to seek answers to these questions is arguably one of the most important factors toward successful execution. In fact, a teacher's deep-rooted willingness and ability to prioritize students' perspectives during learning activities is a crucial starting point (Reeve & Halusic, 2009).

Another significant first step might lead to a bit more discomfort because it requires us to take an honest and reflective look into our existing practices.

While most teachers want to believe that the methods utilized and behaviors modeled are best practices, there can be subtleties that are not as apparent unless genuine introspection takes place. Taking the opportunity to reflect on one's own practices will allow for deeper levels of understanding related to support of students as it relates to autonomy, competence, and relatedness. The table presented in the last chapter (see *Characteristics of Autonomy-Supportive and Controlling-Motivating Styles*) can serve as a starting point for such an evaluation.

SUPPORT OF STUDENT AUTONOMY

Student autonomy is often impeded when pressure-laden teacher practices and coercive language are used to impose a particular set of beliefs, thoughts, or behaviors on students. This often denies students the opportunity to realize their goals, values, and interests (Reeve, 2009; Niemec & Ryan, 2009; Assor et al., 2002). One such prominent example of pressure-laden practices is the required use of results-based, high-stakes testing. While teachers have little to no control over required testing, there remain other opportunities for teachers to apply autonomy-supportive strategies while also meeting curricular demands.

One such way is to provide students with understandable and meaningful rationales regarding daily instructional activities and expectations. Moreover, fostering relevance, providing choice, and allowing for criticism/encouraging independent thinking are paramount to supporting students (Assor et al., 2002). While the last two statements provide generalizations related to implementing autonomy-supportive strategies, it might remain unclear how such approaches could practically serve teachers.

Some teachers tend to feel greater comfort related to specific aspects of autonomy support while feeling uncomfortable in other facets (Stefanou et al., 2004). That is both acceptable and understandable. To unpack some of the strategies that teachers can apply, the same authors identified three features of autonomy support: (a) organizational, (b) procedural, and (c) cognitive. Table 7.1 provides practical strategies that can be implemented immediately in K-12 classes.

Some of these practices are likely already a part of daily routines. What is important to note is that teachers can be autonomy supportive even if they do not apply all the strategies listed above. For example, allowing students to choose their seating arrangements might not be an approach that you are willing to implement. Perhaps you find yourself reviewing the list and find

Table 7.1 Practical Strategies to Support Student Autonomy

Organizational	Procedural	Cognitive
Students are given opportunities to:	Students are given opportunities to:	Students are given opportunities to:
• Choose group members	• Discuss their wants	• Be independent problem-solvers with scaffolding
• Take responsibility for due dates	• Choose the way competence will be demonstrated	• Debate ideas freely
• Choose evaluation procedures	• Choose materials to use in class activities and projects	• Ask questions
• Participate and create classroom rules		• Have less teacher talk time and more teaching listening time
• Choose seating arrangements	• Display their work in individualistic ways	• Discuss multiple approaches and strategies

Source: Adapted from the works of Stefanou et al. (2004).

out that your greater strengths lie in one or more categories. Again, that is more than acceptable in terms of providing students with the autonomy support that they need to achieve.

Supporting students' autonomy in the classroom can present a host of benefits. In some ways, it can create a chain reaction. Students who can exercise their agency in the learning environment show a greater likelihood to perform in a more self-determined manner. Moreover, they are more likely to persevere on tasks that they perceive to be both meaningful and challenging because the task itself is presented as the reward. In other words, the motivation that is driving students is intrinsic in nature.

Thus, in many ways, supporting students' autonomy can serve as the springboard to also supporting and promoting their competence and relatedness. In the middle column above, competence most neatly aligns with aspects of procedural autonomy. In these cases where students can have ownership in the way(s) in which they work through, manipulate, and share their knowledge in ways that are important to them, their psychological need for competence will also be supported.

SUPPORT OF STUDENT COMPETENCE

The need to feel competent can revolve around competency in interpersonal relationships, tasks and activities, and the larger educational environment (Schunk et al., 2008). In order to support students' need for competence, they need to be introduced to learning activities that are challenging and that allow for the expansion of their academic capabilities. Students' competence can also be supported through strategies that align with cognitive autonomy support. To feel competent, students should be provided with the latitude to explore the content and their educational surroundings. Thus, they need to have opportunities to serve as independent problem-solvers with an appropriate amount of scaffolding from their teachers and classmates.

Moreover, students must be provided with meaningful feedback regarding their progress toward a specified task or goal. What is more important is/are the method(s) by which the feedback is provided. Simply relying on an alphanumeric grade or other notation (e.g., gold star, sticker, stamp, etc.) will not sufficiently provide students with the information required to promote success. In fact, such informational feedback should likely be downplayed in its role as an actual evaluation while "providing relevant information on how to master the tasks at hand" (Niemec & Ryan, 2009).

In this case, two aspects of our instructional strategies will have to be addressed in order to support students' competence. The first includes the types of assessments utilized. In part, this goes back to questions mentioned in the last chapter. Are the tasks and activities provided to students both rigorous and relevant? Will students see them as meaningful and worthy of their time? If not, then the activities and assessments will need to be evaluated for reform. One suggestion includes reviewing the Classroom Assessment Techniques (CATs) that were originally developed by Angelo and Cross (1993). CATs are instructional activities that often decenter the classroom away from the teacher—all while checking for student progress and comprehension as well as mastery.

These unique techniques can help to support students' competence through activities deemed less traditional (e.g., papers, tests, quizzes, etc.). They also show the potential to help students become more cognizant of their strengths and weaknesses related to the content and/or activity. Moreover, they can help teachers develop unique daily cognitive objectives for their students while also supporting their growth and achievement.

The second aspect that will need addressing is the way in which alphanumeric grades and other such evaluative measures are applied. One result of high-stakes testing—whether it be state mandated or as part of AP or IB coursework—is that students are often most concerned about the grade. In fact, it is likely that more than a few times in your career, students have posed a question like, "How do I get an 'A'?" While grades are important metrics for students in terms of overall GPA or future goals and aspirations, it should not serve as the only aspect of learning about which students care.

Supporting student competency will require coupling the alphanumeric grades with meaningful information regarding student progress and work. Providing students with more informational evaluations can also help support their self-efficacy. As such, the more students are made aware of their strengths and weaknesses, the greater their ability to make conscious decisions regarding activities, effort, and persistence. Further, these types of structures for support can help build meaningful relationships between teachers and students.

SUPPORT OF STUDENT RELATEDNESS

Students' need for relatedness speaks to their need to experience a sense of belonging to a group. In classrooms, students clearly have a need—no matter what they might display in terms of affect—to build relationships with classmates and teachers. Circling back to the questions that teachers often ask when evaluating autonomy-supportive strategies, two particularly stand front-and-center. Questions about what to say and how to talk with students can provide support to think through strategies related to enhancing students' relatedness. According to Reeve (2006), four overlapping characteristics must be considered which include attunement, relatedness, supportiveness, and gentle discipline.

Teachers who are attuned to their students attempt to understand the needs and thoughts as well as the feelings of their students. In addition, relatedness is developed when teachers allow for a close and personal dynamic between them and their students. Noddings (1988) describes this relatedness as a teacher's response to the "needs, wants, and initiations" of their students. As a result, the student will recognize and respond to the caring initiative of the teacher. Supportiveness allows for teacher affirmation of the student's capacity while the use of gentle discipline promotes the guidance of students in terms of their ways of thinking and believing (Reeve, 2006).

Relationships that are developed between teachers and students are arguably the most conceptual of the three psychological needs. This is because they are largely based on the perceptions and experiences of both teachers and students. What is clear and evident is that positive and nurturing relationships can serve as a catalyst for student learning and performance. Throughout their educational experience, students are striving to "meet their own fundamental needs to belong, to feel competent, and to feel in control" (Davis & Dague, 2020, p. 156).

While building relationships with students can be complicated, it is a process that is both constant and ever-changing. In this vein, teachers' efforts to provide support occur both in their verbal and non-verbal messaging as well as in the ways in which they employ their instructional practices. This goes back to an earlier statement that focused on whether the tasks asked of students to work on will be perceived as meaningful and worthy of their time. When the answer is *yes* to both, there is an implied understanding that students can develop regarding the belief that their teachers have in them. Discussion-based approaches can, in numerous ways, serve as that conduit to support growth and achievement while also promoting the needs that are so important to each and every student in the classroom.

DISCUSSION PEDAGOGY AND AUTONOMY SUPPORT

As previously mentioned, the promotion of discussion pedagogy is not intended to suggest that teachers' already existing practices should be tossed out in favor of this approach. Discussion pedagogy, like any other authentic approach, is intended to serve as a supplement to already existing practices. It would be unreasonable and harmful to suggest that solely teaching through discussion-based approaches is viable.

Many social studies teachers believe they are using discussions as a method for instruction; however, the engagement that teachers believe they will get from students is often thwarted because the "discussions" are actually more in line with recitation. Classroom discussions "must involve a purposeful exchange of views—a dialogue—among the participants themselves" (Parker, 2001, p. 111). Further, genuine discussions promote an active pursuit of both active speaking and listening.

This leads to an important question. Does proper implementation of discussion pedagogy show a likelihood to support students' autonomy and help to facilitate their intrinsic motivation? Seminars and deliberations will likely promote learning experiences for students that can be characterized in three ways: (a) knowledge-deepening, (b) evidence-oriented, and (c) horizon-broadening (Parker, 2006). Moreover, it shows a significant potential to shift the interpersonal dynamics of the classroom. As such, the roles and responsibilities of teachers and students are reframed where teachers are not serving as the sole gatekeepers of knowledge.

Thinking back to the work of Paulo Freire (2014), traditional teacher-student relationships are steeped in an unspoken hierarchy with clear and obvious power dynamics. His description includes two chief stakeholders with a "narrating Subject (the teacher) and patient, listening objects (the students)" (p. 71). In his previously mentioned banking concept of education, teachers are viewed as providing knowledge to what could be considered empty receptacles (the students) who know nothing. If one's worldview on education aligns with that belief, then it is not hard to imagine why direct instruction might serve as an anchor of their instructional delivery.

Further, such a model reduces any and all opportunities for students to serve as creative entities and to display their knowledge in meaningful ways. It also reduces students' abilities to act upon the knowledge with which they are engaging. Thus, proper implementation can serve as a safeguard to the perpetuation of such marginalizing approaches. Further, such approaches speak to the continued disconnect that exists in social studies education at large.

To begin, discussion pedagogy serves as a vehicle to reduce such authoritarian and teacher-centered classroom dynamics. This is accomplished by providing students with opportunities to exert their will. Their will, in this case, is promoted by giving them a voice related to the texts and questions provided. Given the intellectually rigorous nature of discussions, it is students who will, in many ways, drive the discussion and the ideas being explored. Tacitly, it also mitigates authoritarian learning environments which have shown a strong relationship to lower student achievement.

Where authoritarian environments demonstrate a propensity to increase student anxiety and dependence, student-centered environments utilizing discussion-based approaches allow students to serve as stakeholders of knowledge and the construction of such knowledge. Ultimately, teachers cannot serve as the only intellectual within the classroom (Giroux, 1988; Kincheloe, 2008).

This act, while appearing seemingly minor, is shown to support students' procedural autonomy in that they will be able to make decisions on how materials will be used for the discussion. Additionally, this promotes a more democratic approach to teaching and learning that enables students to seek out more challenging work. It can also increase student enjoyment while supporting students who strive toward deeper conceptual understanding (Harter, 1978; Grolnick & Ryan, 1989; Ryan & Deci, 2000).

The freedom to express thought and opinion can produce learning environments where students' engagement and interests can be fostered. It supports a more student-centered atmosphere that encourages student initiative, nurtures competence, and uses non-controlling, motivating language (Lipstein & Renninger, 2007). Additionally, discussion pedagogy strongly associates with supporting students' cognitive autonomy by encouraging students to take ownership of their learning by asking them to "evaluate their own and others' solutions or ideas" (Logan et al., 1995).

Motivated Teachers Lead to Motivated Students

Unless you have worked as a teacher in K-12 spaces, it is difficult to imagine the challenges and complexities that exist—daily, weekly, monthly, and yearly. Teachers are responsible to various stakeholders, and as such, often feel incredible pressure to meet the multifaceted requirements inherent in their profession. This and previous chapters have touched on the external factors that shape teachers and the decision-making in their respective classrooms. Additionally, many teachers are tired and downtrodden with additional requirements that come their way.

What is known is that teachers have the power to influence the lives of their students. Teachers have the "capacity to create environments that help foster their students' motivation toward learning, which also helps them to achieve their potential" (Pelletier & Rocchi, 2016). Such incredible external pressures can shift teachers' actions in ways that are more controlling-motivating and authoritarian and less autonomy-supportive and democratic. This can range from the tone and tenor taken with students to the instructional methods that are utilized.

Teachers who are motivated to reframe their practices to make them more autonomy-supportive are often concerned about how to speak to, and engage with, students. A place to begin includes taking the time to reflect honestly about existing practices and behaviors. While this might create yet another consideration that needs to be mined, at its very core, autonomy-supportive teachers are respectful of "students' perspectives and initiatives, and the tone is one of understanding" (Reeve, 2016). Students need to believe fully that you are their ally and that you are genuinely willing to do what is necessary to provide them with support. Moreover, it is important to back that up with your tone, words, and actions.

To promote and facilitate students' inner motivations and resources, avoidance of controlling, pressure-laden techniques must be addressed. Again, this is not intended to suggest that being autonomy-supportive is synonymous with being permissive. For any classroom to function smoothly, there must be procedures and protocols in place to support its functionality. Thus, providing students with a rationale for the procedures and protocols utilized is paramount. Table 7.2 is illustrative of some of the main ideas that teachers

Table 7.2 Characteristics of Autonomy-Supportive Techniques

1. Takes the Students' Perspectives
- Invites and welcomes students' input
- Aware of students' needs, goals, preferences, and emotions

2. Vitalizes Students' Inner Motivation
- Piques students' curiosity
- Frames learning activities with students' intrinsic goals

3. Provides Explanations and Rationales
- Provides students with an explanation of "why"
- Uses phrasing such as, "Because . . . ," "The reason is . . . "

4. Uses Non-pressuring, Informational Language
- Provides choices and options
- Teachers are flexible, open-minded, and responsive

5. Displays Patience
- Allows opportunities for students to work at their own pace
- Waits for student signaling of input, initiative, and willingness

Source: Adapted from Reeve (2016).

who want to adopt more autonomy-supportive strategies should consider in their own practice.

Autonomy Support through Discussion-Based Approaches

Aside from managing a class, autonomy-supportive teachers must also consider how their instructional practices impact student motivation. It is evident that strategies that align with Freire's banking concept of education will routinely thwart students' interest and engagement as well as motivation. Such an approach reduces students' need for ownership in their own educational process while also reducing learning to a series of passive transactions where the ends and/or products are all that matter.

Discussion pedagogy presents a supplemental alternative that can shift the landscape from that of transactional to transformational. As Harter and Connell (1984) posit, intrinsic motivation can be based on five assumptions whereby students

- prefer challenging rather than easy work;
- seek to satisfy their own interest and curiosity rather than working to please the teacher;
- desire independent attempts for mastery rather than relying on the teacher;
- want independent judgment rather than only the teacher's judgment; and
- need internal criteria for success and failure rather than external criteria.

These assumptions support and align with the goals and objectives of discussion pedagogy. Moreover, discussion pedagogy clearly aligns with aspects of autonomy support—most specifically in terms of procedural and cognitive autonomy support. It presents an opportunity to decenter the role of the teacher while supporting students' need to co-construct knowledge with their classmates through scaffolded seminars and/or deliberations. It provides students with a voice that they often do not get to share. Moreover, it promotes less teacher talk time and more teacher listening time.

FINAL THOUGHTS

Discussion pedagogy, as a practice of teaching, has shown to have myriad positive impacts on students. The conversation will continue in subsequent chapters about its potentiality. What is clear and evident is that systematically implemented discussion-based approaches—whether it be seminars and/or deliberations—have the potential to motivate students in ways that might not have been previously experienced.

If motivation produces, and if the ultimate goal is to support student growth and achievement, then it is imperative to think through strategies that help students grow and develop. Discussion pedagogy presents moments for students to exert their will and agency in the classroom. Through exploration of meaningful texts and centralizing questions, students will be able to serve as co-constructors of knowledge presented in class. As framed through SDT, the more students can exercise their will, the more their needs and inner motivation will be facilitated.

Further, as social studies teachers, if the overarching objective is to help support students' understandings of how to engage in their future democratic and civic lives, discussion pedagogy instructs them how to engage with various stakeholders. In part, this is what makes a seminar and/or a deliberation different than a debate. There is no intention for clearly defined winners and losers. Discussions are intended to promote compromise and collaboration. Whether it is intended to promote development of knowledge or engagement as it relates to a collectively identified problem, discussion pedagogy produces such opportunities.

In closing, students need to be encouraged to analyze the possibilities and the social, political, and pedagogical contradictions of schooling (Kincheloe & Steinberg, 1998). Conceptually, the promotion of a problem-posing, dialogically meaningful discourse, and decision-making within a classroom setting can be academically, politically, and socially empowering to students. Teachers need to be systematic in their approach and find ways in which curricula and instructional methods can coalesce to allow for the creation of such a dynamic learning environment. This possibility can be fulfilled through the utilization of more autonomy-supportive motivating strategies—to include discussions and academic discourse.

Chapter 8

The Community

In my first semester in higher education, I was assigned a general methods course for graduate students who were seeking licensure in middle or high school. It was an incredible group of students who came from a variety of backgrounds. The class pushed me to familiarize myself with the curricula for science, mathematics, ELA, and physical education—not just social studies. It was a daunting task for me because I had been so deeply entrenched in social studies education for my entire professional and academic career.

I often proclaimed to students that this class would support their understandings related to day-to-day operational spaces of teaching and learning. We would cover everything from classroom management to the impact of student diversity to lesson planning. In short order, one semester of fifteen class sessions, I was hoping to support the building of new teachers who could go out and serve their young people well—irrespective of the content area. In the opening weeks of the class, maybe our third meeting, I had a student ask me a question that has left a mark on my teaching ever since.

The student's question was in response to a question I asked and that tasked them to write in an introspective and honest way. It asked them to explore what excited them and what they feared the most about entering the classroom as a student- or first-year teacher. Through the candid back-and-forth that followed, one student asked me, "What do you think are the characteristics that signal an effective teacher?" I remember pausing for a second to make sure that I could, based on my experiences and research, answer the question in a concise and efficient way.

What was borne out of that question is what I often refer to as the "Four Pillars of Effective Teachers." First, teachers need to know their content. Knowing the content, even those topics that give us trouble, is an imperative to opening the opportunities related to how that knowledge can be shared with students in meaningful and authentic ways. In essence, the more comfortable teachers are with the content, the more likely they are to challenge themselves and their students beyond mere memorization and recitation.

Second, teachers must focus on having a flawless, but flexible, plan for classroom management. Pushing beyond thinking about classroom management as simply rules and consequences, teachers need to develop plans for a litany of possibilities that might arise in their classes. From procedures for accepting late work to administering tests and quizzes, teachers need to have a plan that is carefully thought out and developed.

Third, teachers need to produce thoughtful instructional design. Distilled down, they need to create lessons and plans that help students achieve, develop, and grow. With that end in mind, teachers must ask themselves how their instructional activities provide engaging learning opportunities for their students.

While these "pillars" are not intended to be hierarchical, I intentionally leave this one last. In all methods courses I have taught since that night, I simply say that the fourth characteristic is "to love those kids." Extrapolated, I routinely follow up by explaining how powerful the relationships in any classroom can be and the impact that they can have on students—now and in their future lives. Building relationships with students should be viewed in a multidirectional manner, not simply between teachers and students but also between/among the students themselves.

These meaningful relationships can be supported and manifested only when students have opportunities to interact as part of the thoughtful instructional design that is being utilized. The more students participate in their own learning and construct meaning from content that minimizes the overreliance on direct instruction, the more students can cultivate such relationships. It is evident that utilizing discussion pedagogy and its alignment to promote open discourse—for knowing and/or political engagement—can support the cultivation of such relationships. The more in-depth and well-developed these relationships become, the greater the potential for your classrooms to be akin to that of learning communities.

DISCUSSION PEDAGOGY AND SOCIAL CONSTRUCTIVISM

Education prep programs routinely introduce new theories and concepts related to teaching and learning in K-12 spaces. To be effective teachers, there is much value placed on understanding some of the theories contained within the profession at large. Where theories often lose their impact in such programs is when there is difficulty in making the connection between conceptual understanding and practical application. Understanding for meaningful use must be couched in ways that support pre- and in-service teachers' work with their students.

When the connection between theory and praxis can be made, a sort of idealistic excitement can be created that allows us to think about its potential in the classroom. Being both idealistic and optimistic signals a belief that you can serve as an agent of change. The realities of time and other instructional constraints can lead to a path of losing that feeling of becoming a changemaker which often results in a reversion back to a sort of status quo. One such act of reversal can lead to, once again, becoming overly reliant on more commonly accepted practices such as direct instruction. To reiterate, direct instruction is a viable instructional approach to teaching and learning social studies; however, its viability can quickly diminish if not coupled with instructional strategies deemed more active and engaging.

The benefits of utilizing discussions in social studies classes are plentiful. That much is clear, and while assuredly biased on that front, there is evidence to suggest that discussion pedagogy can help build a community of learners in social studies classrooms. More to come on that later. For now, it is also deeply important to recognize how it parallels and intersects with some of the idealistic and engaging theories mentioned earlier.

In thinking about ways to decenter the classroom away from teachers and toward students, discussions are pedagogically sound in their promotion of social constructivism. Often linked to theories developed by Piaget and Vygotsky, *constructivism* focuses on how students actively construct and make meaning of their understanding and knowledge. *Social constructivism* narrows the scope by emphasizing the social contexts of learning and how knowledge is mutually developed and constructed. Social constructivist approaches promote that students are exposed to others' ways of thinking as they create a shared understanding (Santrock, 2020). Thus, it is clear to see how the principles of discussion pedagogy could neatly intersect those of social constructivism.

Further, social constructivism promotes that social interaction plays an integral role in student learning. Social interaction that takes place in the classroom allows students to learn from both the teacher and each other (Blake & Pope, 2008). The concept of learning from both the teacher and classmates perfectly aligns with the objectives of discussion pedagogy—in this case, specifically seminars. The promotion of enlightenment allows students to engage with the content, and each other, in ways that might not occur as organically or effectively with other teacher-centered approaches.

Thinking through discussion-based approaches and their benefits is one thing. That is the exciting part, especially when thinking about how students might respond and begin to engage with the material, and each other, differently. The brass tacks part of the process, especially when thinking how it aligns with concepts related to social constructivism, is equally as critical to the success of such approaches.

In thinking through Vygotsky's work, there is the belief that students can learn more and behave in more engaged ways when afforded opportunities to work in co-constructive ways. Discussions allow for students to work, not only with teachers, but with classmates in a socially interactive fashion, and with potentially more skilled students, to move their learning along. What Vygotsky refers to as the Zone of Proximal Development (ZPD) allows for students to receive assistance and support from their classmates. What makes the intersection of ZPD and classroom discussions unique is the fact that the assistance and support occurs in more natural ways.

Classroom discussions provide opportunities for students to think through new material being presented based on the meaningful texts and central questions that are provided. With the time provided to students to develop their thoughts, they could also be given opportunities to work with their classmates via individualized scaffolding, small groups, or through cooperative learning (Blake & Pope, 2008). All the prep work that students can accomplish together will then be fleshed out through the active speaking and listening that will take place during the discussion itself. In essence, the cooperative measures being developed and employed to support student learning prior to the discussion will likely be accelerated during the discussion. Instructional activities need to empower students to create meaning through intentional manipulation of the material with which they are working (Blake & Pope, 2008; Fogerty, 1999).

One of the points of grounding discussion pedagogy in theory is that it exemplifies yet another reason to consider its usage in social studies classrooms. When authentic and innovative practices are presented for potential implementation, there will be those who question their viability in terms of promoting student performance and achievement. The clearly delineated intersections will serve as another support to promote the strategic use of such an approach. The more that students can learn, and create meaning, from each other, the more this approach will provide them countless added benefits. In addition to the benefit of performance, students will be able to engage in a classroom learning environment that is based on cooperation and community.

DISCUSSIONS AND COMMUNITY

Discussions present a sort of power and ownership that students often do not receive in their learning experiences. The need for ownership and agency in one's learning environment is one that promotes students' intrinsic motivation. Again, this is not to deride the amazing work that so many teachers do, but the constrained professionalism that many teachers experience tends to naturally manifest itself in the styles and practices that teachers tend to implement. Discussions present students with an opportunity to take on new roles and responsibilities in their learning, and, as such, they will likely begin to prepare for these discussions in very different ways.

As part of any discussion, students are explicitly and/or implicitly provided with meaningful choices and options which enhance their practices toward preparation. As students enhance and improve their self-regulatory behaviors, there is a sense of confidence that will grow. Such growth can be enhanced through their participation in the discussions—especially when teachers and classmates behave in some of the autonomy-supportive ways mentioned in an earlier chapter. The strategies that can be most effective toward developing a community of learners through discussions include the following: (1) using non-controlling language, (2) providing instructional patience, and (3) sharing acceptance of students' expressions. While the first two strategies often land squarely on the shoulders of teachers, the last rests in the control of all stakeholders.

This is where earlier discussions related to teaching, modeling, and scaffolding skills related to active speaking and active listening come into play. As students grow in confidence—both in themselves and in the experiences in which they are participating—they are likely to perceive a degree of satisfaction that will likely dictate their intrinsic motivation. Ultimately, the hope is that these experiences will occur in a sort of recursive loop. With every positive experience they have with discussion-based approaches, their growth and development will springboard in very meaningful and unique ways.

Creating a learning environment in which students feel comfortable is imperative to both student performance and achievement. While mentioned on several occasions, when students are relegated to environments where they experience passivity, they might not feel as if their voices matter. Such subordination and passivity will likely cause many students to feel indifferent toward participation. Discussions and dialogue have the potential to engage even the most quiet and reserved students. In some cases, their inability to participate in instructional activities that are authentic and engaging can create uncertainty when students are afforded such an opportunity. Students have mentioned, in previous research, that part of the reason they maintained their reserved style and demeanor is because they did not want to look *wrong* in front of their classmates (Dague, 2015).

This fear of looking *wrong* or *stupid* in front of their classmates is yet another reason why discussions can support student performance and achievement. With the central question being intellectually challenging and open to interpretation, there should not necessarily be a prescribed *right* or *wrong* response. This is written to suggest that building such a community will take time, so patience is assuredly a virtue in this case. While students, and teachers for that matter, appreciate the comfort of lectures and more directive approaches, the more students are exposed to discussions, the more they will gain comfort in the process and with their classmates. In part, this happens because students are likely to recognize how seminars and deliberations can help them go in more depth related to the materials and the content.

Helping to build the community will also take work on your part. To build a community, it is necessary to be mindful of not allowing small groups of students to dominate the conversation. In some cases, it might be necessary to use gentle redirection to help others feel included in the discussion. In helping those students who do not have the natural inclination to participate, the community of learners can grow.

As students get more engaged in the process, many of them will likely begin to enhance their practice toward preparation. As their preparation improves, which research has shown is likely to happen, they will naturally gain more comfort (Dague, 2015). This, in part, leads back to the importance of text(s) selection and question(s) development. When students begin doing their own additional search on the topics in preparation for the discussion, many will do so to develop a deeper level of understanding that they will then be able to use in the discussion. Organically, students will begin to worry more about the process of learning and less about the grades associated with participation. As such, this creates a shift away from being solely concerned about the product and more focused on the process. As students' preparation and participation improves, many will begin to participate because they want to be involved, having developed a deeper level of interest and engagement.

Additionally, building a community of learners will likely happen, not only in times of agreement, but also in times of contention regarding classmates' thoughts. A great example of this occurred in a pilot study from a few years ago. The content being addressed focused on imperialism in the nineteenth century. One student (Alexander)[1] spoke about how it is unfair of us in the twenty-first century to "vilify" the colonizers being discussed. After the student's position was made, in my field notes, I wrote that "the air just got sucked out of the room." The point he was making is one that is often made by historians as it relates to historical presentism. However, his classmates still found his point troublesome. Perhaps it was his tone or tenor, but it was clear that it struck a nerve.

Another student (Elizabeth), who did not participate as frequently in the seminars, jumped right in explaining how she disagreed with aspects of the concept her classmate presented. Her willingness to put herself out there and to disagree required tremendous nerve given the fact that the notes reflected that her voice was "trembling as she shared her personal statement." This presents a larger benefit. It is often much easier to participate in challenging discussions when you align with the opinion of the majority or when you agree with what has recently been stated. Running counter to the opinions of classmates and peer groups can be troubling—especially as students get older and their relationships to those in school grow more important.

A community of learners is truly developed when students feel comfortable and free to agree *and* disagree with their classmates. While nervous and uneasy about how her thoughts might be received, Elizabeth felt comfortable enough to disagree with her classmate. She did not stop there. She continued to expound on her ideas and questioned our role in trying to make profound change in our society. In a post-observation interview, Elizabeth discussed how she was proud of herself for putting her thoughts out there for others to hear. She explained that when she heard others agree with her thoughts, that gave her more confidence to speak out in the future.

Enhancing students' confidence and comfort will help to facilitate the building of a community of learners, which should be an intended goal. While it might feel like this example is more of an outlier than the norm, experience and research show that students truly want to be heard and that they want the opportunity to share ideas with their teachers and classmates. With increased comfort comes increased participation. This participation can be experienced without the use of formative assessment and rubrics.

In another class, the sense of community began to grow as students gained a greater sense of relatedness to their classmates and the teacher. Another student, Nicholas, explained in his interview that he felt far more comfortable saying what was on his mind. He explained that "you always have that insecurity with what you know and what others are going to judge you upon . . . and how you feel about a subject."

While seminars and deliberations are intended to create opportunities for students to cooperate with one another, there will be moments where the competitive juices will amplify. Some students will become competitive, not in the way of wanting to win a debate, but there becomes a sort of ingrained competition with being more prepared to be even more participatory. This could be explained in many ways. What likely causes this is the fact that students truly believe they are in command of the trajectory and flow of the classroom. This competition, for one student, was about being prepared to the point where she could listen to others and then develop "better questions" that could be used to spur on the conversation.

Two other interviews pointed to how community development intersected between the balance of competition and cooperation. One student spoke about the unique opportunity for her and her classmates:

I think it feels really nice because a lot of people don't like to take that step. I think a class which does that, they're going to learn more. I think it helped us to get closer in that sense and also just to broaden [our] understanding and just think that it's okay that I'm different. It's okay that I have the same opinion. It makes you more open-minded to different suggestions going on.

Another student focused his response on how it was unique to actually learn from his classmates:

You [the teacher] would ask a question that was very important to the conversation and then the teacher let us take it away. I think we kind of taught ourselves sometimes. . . . It was back-and-forth, and I would learn from other students. It's just weird to think about you learning from your peers along with learning from your teachers.

So much of the data and research show that by implementing discussion-based approaches, student involvement will be impacted, and part of that impact surrounds the communal learning environments that can be created. The development of such communal learning environments, through free and open discourse, provides students with opportunities to increase their agency within the learning environment. With a shift in agency, students will be able to freely express their thoughts in the discussions and in their responses to the central questions. Further, providing students with the opportunity to actively participate in the learning environment in a way that is "consistent with their goals and interests" can pave the way for students to engage with others more frequently and thoughtfully, thus building a community-based experience (Assor et al., 2002).

DISCUSSIONS AND SUPPORT OF RELATEDNESS

In review, the principles of self-determination theory posit that students, and really all of us, have three innate psychological needs that require support. While the catalyst of these needs comes through support of student autonomy, students also require support and promotion of their relatedness. Support of students' relatedness can not only be fulfilled by their teachers and classmates but can also be supported and satisfied by the relevance of the content being learned.

The pressure that students experience in social studies classes, due in part to summative, high-stakes tests, can make them feel a sense of discontent in the learning environment. This rings especially true when direct instruction is the primary method of instruction. Given the pressures that exist in our current testing-frenzied educational climate, students are likely to feel as if they are just another number seeking to achieve a grade. With the breadth-depth issues that teachers face in terms of time and space, there can be many situations where students' learning experiences are stifled because of an unwillingness to take time to address questions and ideas that students present in class.

Naturally, such an unwillingness can thwart students' relatedness to the teacher, fellow classmates, and the learning environment at large. Moreover, relatedness can be frustrated, which, in turn, can prevent students from meeting their learning goals. In cases where discussion pedagogy is implemented, students' need for relatedness is more likely to be supported when their values and ideas can be exchanged free of any external controls, pressures, and/or measures. As Niemec and Ryan (2009) present, students "tend to internalize and accept as their own the values and practices of those they feel, or want to feel, connected, and... experience a sense of belonging" (p. 139).

The implementation of discussion pedagogy can also create a more authentic teacher-student relationship by altering the hierarchy within the learning environment. When the predominant method of instructional delivery is based on teacher-centered instructional methods, there is an implied understanding that the teacher serves as the sole gatekeeper of information.

While some students might perceive the use of lectures positively, it can create a divide between teachers and students. For other students, it can also create a divide between them and the content. Interactions between teachers and students "may shape students' social motivational beliefs and, in turn, their beliefs about their academic and social competence, their values, and their pursuit of academic and social goals in the classroom" (Davis, 2003, p. 209).

Unsurprisingly, stand-and-deliver methods demonstrate lower support for students' autonomy. Discussion pedagogy demonstrates an opportunity to reduce some of the hierarchical barriers that might exist for some of the students in your classes. In changing their perceived roles, through an increase in agency, students were able to engage with classmates more frequently and organically. Going back to "Nicholas," he discussed how the normal breakdown of the class was lectures filled with some back-and-forth volleying of questions. After a more routine implementation of both seminars and deliberations, Nicholas wrote:

> I felt a lot more active and a lot more ready to be able to say what was on my mind, and it seemed like my classmates were [as well]. A lot more people began speaking up, and when it carried on between student-and-student discussion more than [between] student and teacher, it felt like we were leading everything.

Perhaps one of the most powerful statements came from a student who elucidated that, because of the discussions, she no longer felt as if "the teacher is God, and we are just a bunch of grunt students." This statement should lead us to question just how many more of our students feel the very same way. While not intentional, it is evident that certain instructional methods used can negatively impact the relationships that can be built in our classes.

Discussion pedagogy can create an understanding between the teacher and students in terms of power sharing in the class. Students became aware of the repositioning of their role in the class. One student interviewed pointed out that students were able to ask questions of each other, and they eventually felt as if they were becoming the "[the teacher] of the classroom." This statement demonstrates what an empowering experience this created.

Another student felt as if the teacher in the study treated her and her classmates in a more adult-like manner, which she welcomed. While some students felt as if the teacher had already treated them in an adult-like manner, there was a sense that they truly rose to an equal footing. This student followed up, "It [discussion pedagogy] was different because when [the teacher] was doing lectures and stuff it was quite obvious they were the leader of it. When we went to seminars, it felt like myself and three other people were the leaders . . . and [the teacher] was just kind of the sheep herder." This, among other things, demonstrates the enhanced degree of both autonomy and relatedness that students experienced.

FINAL THOUGHTS

The very best of us work diligently on our craft. There is hard work being done to know the content and to find ways to engage the students. In thinking about the benefits of conducting cooperative learning experiences, we might often feel forced in the way that we are just trying to give our students another option for learning the same materials. Discussions open avenues for students to not only explore the material but to also gain insight into each other. Conceptually, learning with and from each other seems like a reasonable approach to help engage students in the material being delivered.

What makes these types of environments special is the organic nature with which students can take ownership of their own learning. These opportunities shift the landscape of the classroom and the hierarchy that often exists within it. John Dewey (2009) wrote that the "measure of the value of an experience lies in the perception of relationships." The building and cultivation of positive and binding relationships can impact the trajectory of students' lives in numerous ways. While learning the prescribed material is important, the experiences that students have through that process can support or thwart those learning outcomes.

While power dynamics must exist as it relates to managing a class and setting up its rules and procedures to make sure that classrooms operate smoothly, the learning process should be a truly shared experience. In the process of co-constructing knowledge, we learn as much about ourselves as we do about the material. Further, both teachers and students learn even more about the people in their classes who impact their lives daily. The promotion of co-construction levels the playing field between teachers and students. It gives potential to reduce the impediments to growth and development between teachers and students.

Again, Dewey's (2009) work supports this in the sense that the very term *pupil* has become synonymous with not engaging in "fruitful experiences but absorbing knowledge directly." Whether it be Vygotsky or Dewey or Freire, rethinking the dynamics of our classrooms can come through authentic approaches to teaching and learning. When meaningful learning opportunities are experienced by teachers and students alike, the community can take shape and develop. Once that community takes shape, opportunities for growth and achievement will be boundless.

NOTE

1. All names used are pseudonyms to maintain anonymity of the students.

Chapter 9

The Skills

In the opening weeks of my methods courses, my students are asked to develop a one-to-two-page statement of philosophy related to teaching. Treating this as an iterative assignment requires students to make any necessary changes, based on the feedback provided, before they can complete the course. While it might be viewed as a potentially antiquated assignment, I believe it serves a few important purposes.

First, it helps me evaluate what candidates believe are the important facets of their chosen profession. Their work provides me with an avenue to get at the heart of why they want to be teachers. It also operates as a diagnostic assessment of sorts. It helps me identify where students "are" related to their understanding of the profession. Depending on where they are in the program and their professional experiences, students' responses often vary. More on this in a moment.

Second, conceivably more pragmatic in nature, this document helps them with both their application process and future interviews with prospective employers. If asked, I want them to be prepared with a flawless document that hopefully sets them apart from the competition. I always discuss with them that it is important to not "bury the lead." In this case, it is important to come out firing on all cylinders to ensure that the principal and/or assistant principal reading it likes what is being shared from the very beginning.

Last, it is to provide them with a meaningful opportunity to be reflective and introspective. The profession of serving as a K-12 teacher, social studies or otherwise, is one filled with countless challenges and unknowns. The highs and lows of being a teacher make this profession so incredibly unique and fulfilling. As a result, I want them to have a moment to think carefully through their respective beliefs. In most semesters, I share a copy of my very first statement of philosophy from my undergrad days. I do so to share with them how what we think we know upon entering the profession will likely change as we grow in our experience as professional educators. Mine certainly has over the last twenty years.

All of this is written to point out one thing that seems to be constant when I read through the initial drafts of these statements. Nearly all students write about pushing their students to develop many of the skills that they will need now and in their future lives. They write about how they hope to create a learning environment that promotes their students' critical thinking. Moreover, they routinely mention phrases that revolve around helping students to "think outside of the box." While I love to read this, it also causes me a bit of trepidation.

My concern is rooted in the fact that when I push them to flesh out what they conceive as critical thinking and how their practices will help promote these skills, there is often a lack of clarity and understanding in their responses. As such, these skills get added to a larger bucket of educational buzzwords. To promote their growth and understanding in this area, throughout the remainder of the semester, we routinely revisit the ideas surrounding "skills" so that students can better identify and understand the instructional practices they can employ to promote their future students' growth and development.

In part, that is what this chapter is here to help support. While it is much more comfortable to revert back to stand-and-deliver methods with PowerPoint presentations, it should cause us to reckon with how our practices actually minimize students' opportunities to develop their skills. The focus, in this case, is about the skills associated with social studies education. One such skill that discussion pedagogy is clearly linked to is the promotion of historical argumentation. What's more, by employing strategies and methods related to discussion pedagogy, students will be exposed and pushed to develop and enhance their soft skills. Soft skills, such as communication, problem-solving, and critical thinking, neatly align with practices associated with meaningful and authentic discussions in social studies classes.

MEANINGFUL THINKING

While the term "thinking" seems simple enough, the myriad facets and considerations that exist, as it relates to teaching and learning, are anything but simple. Santrock (2020) defines the term as that which "involves manipulating and transforming information in memory." The ideas surrounding manipulation and transforming information should jump right off the page for every social studies teacher. This means that if the goal is to promote meaningful thinking in social studies classes—regardless of what type of thinking it is—students must participate in instructional exercises that allow them to both manipulate and transform the content being learned.

Even if the instructional exercises are not discussion-based, this should reaffirm the realization that a teachers' instructional design needs to be centered on students and their ability to have ownership and autonomy. Providing transformational learning opportunities not only promotes students' thinking, but it also demonstrates linkages to democratic practices that align with the goals of social studies education. Further, when students are provided opportunities to be in control of their learning, they are naturally more inclined to generate and create a more well-rounded understanding of the topics being learned (Jung & Avolio, 1999).

If such instructional activities are limited, then how can teachers truly expect that their students will grow and develop their skills related to thinking? Moreover, meaningful thinking needs to be pushed beyond the active verbs associated with Bloom's Taxonomy. While terms such as reasoning, conceptualizing, creating, and deciding are fine for writing cognitive instructional objectives, they can only be actualized when teachers provide students with learning opportunities that are congruent.

Such opportunities for meaningful thinking can be experienced when students are able to think critically and creatively, make decisions, and solve problems. What is hopefully clear at this point is that there are obvious parallels that can be drawn between the skills associated with thinking and those of discussion-based approaches. In fact, both seminars and deliberations present moments for students to think critically while also being able to make decisions and solve problems.

PROMOTING SOFT SKILLS

It might seem easier to begin with the thinking skills related directly to history and the social studies, but in the spirit of aligning our practices to the larger goals of social studies education, it might be more prudent to identify how discussions can support students' development of their soft skills. Implementing discussions in classes has numerous "in the moment" benefits. That being said, it is important to also project how utilizing discussions can also support students in their future lives.

The ubiquity of technology, with all that it has to offer, has also presented a generation or so of students who might struggle to communicate and interact with those around them in the moment. In fact, the near-constant evolution of technology will likely cause future generations to have to work together in new and unique ways. This means that they will need to work on, and refine, their respective soft skills.

Soft skills, or interpersonal skills, are a "set of personal attributes and abilities that allow individuals to effectively interact with others in a professional setting [which includes] the ability to navigate complex interpersonal dynamics and build strong relationships" (Danao, 2023). The ability to work effectively with others is something that future employers will assuredly value. Such an ability can be supported through instructional delivery via discussions in our classrooms.

Some of these valuable soft skills have been discussed in previous chapters. For instance, in every list reviewed for use in this chapter, at or near the top, was the ability to communicate. More specifically, communication can be delivered verbally or in a written fashion. On the list provided by Danao (2023), under communication, the traits included are as follows: (1) active listening, (2) verbal and non-verbal communication, (3) written communication, and (4) presentation skills. Active listening, which was covered in detail earlier, was situated at the top of the list, signaling the value of making sure that you are positioning students to be successful—now and for the long term.

Two other soft skills showed an evident linkage to the skills associated with discussion pedagogy. On that same list of eleven, as well as all of the other lists reviewed, critical thinking showed up time and again. Again, the promotion of critical thinking leads to helping students think outside of the box. Also, under the domain of *leadership*, problem-solving was listed at the top of the examples. Problem-solving is just one of many important skills related to leadership, but it is clear that enhancing students' problem-solving skills is paramount to achievement and overall success. Once again, it is clear how effective discussions can support our students.

Critical Thinking

While it has been mentioned several times throughout the book, this is yet another perfect moment to evaluate how your practices can mitigate the discord between the rhetoric and reality of social studies education. This discord, in part, stems from the long-standing debate as to whether "schools should direct their efforts to teaching students *how* to think rather than *what* to think" (Bruning et al., 2011). Going back to the idea of pushing that proverbial envelope, it is important to know that helping students with their skills related to critical thinking is complex in its focus on students being able to identify and evaluate information.

If critical thinking involves students thinking reflectively and productively as they evaluate evidence, then practices associated with discussion-based approaches appear to clearly align (Santrock, 2020). The very processes associated with seminars neatly align with students needing to behave reflectively. Whether that reflective practice is part of their preparation of resources and materials or their participation in the discussion itself, the need to be open to available information and others' ideas can stoke critical thinking.

Preparation for, and participation in, discussions also promotes one other significant aspect of critical thinking. Discussions can help students develop their abilities related to being more mindful. As a key to critical thinking, mindful students can "create new ideas, are open to new information, and are aware of more than one perspective" (Santrock, 2020). Thus, strategically using discussions can open students up to ideas and opportunities that more directive practices simply cannot.

Conceptually, the connections are right in front of us. If students are truly to become more critical and mindful thinkers, implementing discussion-based approaches can help support that endeavor. The presentation of new and meaningful texts exposes them to new information that they otherwise might not get from a more traditional textbook. Coupled with a central question that promotes the *why* and *how* as opposed to just the *what* will naturally provide them with moments to engage with numerous perspectives. In the end, they will have a greater potential to generate their own ideas and ways of thinking to support and drive the discussion itself.

While the connections are clear, it is important that the structure and delivery of such discussions are pedagogically sound. This is not only important for the growth and development of critical thinking skills, but it is also imperative to ensure that students are properly engaged with the content. Skills associated with critical thinking can be promoted as part of any lesson plan. Again, what is clear is that there are ostensible intersections that exist with the discussion-based approaches. Those practices include helping students to

- focus on the *how* and *why*, in addition to the *what*;
- state responses in reasoned and measured ways rather than solely based on emotional responses;
- recognize that there are moments where more than one answer exists;
- evaluate and question others' responses in lieu of accepting an answer as the truth; and
- ask questions that push to potentially create new ideas and information (Santrock, 2020).

Critical thinking entails not only a critical examination of beliefs (i.e., enlightenment) but also potential courses of action (i.e., engagement). Work by Ennis (1987) further supports and corroborates these connections. He identified twelve abilities associated with critical thinking. While all twelve could further push the narrative that discussions serve as meaningful opportunities to promote students' critical thinking, there were six that stood out. They included students' (1) focusing on a question, (2) analyzing arguments, (3) asking and answering questions for clarification, (4) judging the credibility of the sources, (5) deciding on an action, and (6) interacting with others. Ultimately, in order to move *critical thinking* out of the bucket of educational buzzwords, consideration must be given to what it is and how instructional practices either promote or impede students' progress and development.

Problem-Solving

Enhancing students' problem-solving abilities is something on which all teachers focus their attention in the classroom. Problem-solving, as it relates to discussion pedagogy, most closely aligns with deliberative instructional practices. Again, deliberations can be used to help students collaborate in ways to identify an appropriate solution(s) to an established, shared problem. In terms of social studies education, this allows students to think and engage politically.

Problem-solving can be most challenging in the sense that the identification *and* articulation of the problem can be troubling. The problems that discussions can present to students, or that students can identify, need to be relevant to their lives. A more real-world approach must be taken as opposed to providing students with a cookie-cutter problem that has a clearly defined solution (Radvansky & Ashcraft, 2018). Bruning et al. (2011) corroborate this point by writing that "problem discovery is the most crucial stage of the problem-solving sequence."

In relation to discussion pedagogy, and deliberative exercises specifically, it is important for teachers to not allow the problems being presented to spiral out of control. Thus, helping students to evaluate potential solutions as part of the deliberation is important. Again, this demonstrates another example of how important the scaffolding process is in the discussion-based opportunities presented to students. There is a certain striking that must be created in which help is provided to a certain point in the process.

After identifying the shared problem and reviewing the meaningful texts provided or collected by students, developing an initial solution is an important next step. However, the deliberative process can only support students' problem-solving skills if they are allowed to probe and interrogate the viability and potential effectiveness of the solution itself. As part of this step, it will likely lead students to contend with other potential issues that might arise given the solution. This is the point at which you might need to interject to keep students in line and on track. Similar to your own experiences in school, it is quite easy to end up down various rabbit holes.

It is important to recognize that working to enhance students' problem-solving skills through deliberative practices can have some obstacles. Three specific obstacles include the following: (1) fixation, (2) lack of motivation, and (3) inadequate emotional control (Santrock, 2020). Students can become fixated on a particular way to solve the shared problem. As such, they can refuse to consider any of the other available options that are being presented to them by their classmates. Redirecting students, as a method for scaffolding, is important if you see students' fixations getting in the way of the larger goals of the class.

Solving problems can present a host of challenges for students. If students have a diminished view of their ability to solve problems, even with the help of their classmates, they might go into a metaphoric shell. When this becomes apparent, helping to redirect students will be important—especially if they have shown previously to regress when challenges arise. This aligns with previous mentions about how a student's self-efficacy can impact his or her ability to persist when facing obstacles.

Lacking emotional control is something everyone struggles with at times. However, in a deliberation when potentially controversial topics and problems are being addressed, this can be exacerbated by some students who struggle more than most. Again, using a variety of scaffolding techniques can remind and support students to pause and think about their reactions before they broadcast their responses in visceral ways.

The parallels between discussion pedagogy and the development of students' skills appear to have significant connectivity. While some ambiguity might still exist, it is clear that the skills associated with active listening from chapter 5, as well as critical thinking and problem-solving, have merit as they relate to implementing discussion-based approaches. Moreover, discussions in the classroom also show connections toward enhancing students' historical thinking skills and other associated skills needed to be effective learners of the social studies.

HISTORICAL THINKING

Oftentimes, meaningful thoughts and thinking in social studies education revolve around what is often termed "historical thinking skills." While social studies education goes far beyond just the teaching and learning of history, it is clear when looking through state-prescribed curricula that history might still serve as the de facto anchor of social studies education. While some might shirk that notion, it is neither a new debate nor one that is necessary for the points that will be shared in this chapter.

This is not intended to discount the importance of understanding what historical thinking skills include. In fact, according to The College Board (2013), the governing body for Advanced Placement (AP) courses, identifies four historical thinking skills that need to be addressed and integrated into AP history courses; those include the following: (1) chronological reasoning, (2) comparison and contextualization, (3) crafting historical arguments from historical evidence, and (4) historical interpretation and synthesis.

Going back to the article with which chapter 1 opened, Peter Stearns (1998) makes several cases for the importance of history and the benefits that it presents. In his article, "Why Study History?" he presents three skills that students of history can develop. While social studies is more than just history, it is clear that these skills are transcendent, whether learning history or one of the other disciplines that make up the social studies. The skills that Stearns (1998) posits include the

- ability to assess evidence;
- ability to assess conflicting interpretations; and
- experience in assessing past examples of change.

One point that he also makes that is of particular importance in relation to discussion pedagogy is the ability to comb through and utilize different kinds of evidence. There is an important, but possibly underlying, point in this statement. The implication is that social studies teachers need to share multiple sources, and types of sources, with students. Simply put, it is time to move beyond the comforts of the textbook and help students to experience the richness of other sources that exist.

If it has been mentioned once, it has been mentioned dozens of times. When identifying meaningful texts, considering the rigor and relevance of the sources being selected is imperative. What's more, the need to consider the form it takes is equally important. It is not necessary to jump straight into lengthy primary sources. While rigorous, it might end up lacking the relevancy that will pique students' interest and, consequently, diminish their engagement. Thus, the only way to support such skills is to work diligently in the selection of the meaningful texts that will serve to anchor the discussion.

Stearns' (1998) point that students will be given the chance to assess conflicting viewpoints takes on a couple of different layers. In relation to discussion pedagogy, students will be afforded the opportunity to not only learn from the texts and resources provided, but they will be exposed to varying perspectives and vantage points of their classmates. One of the important facets of serving as both an active discussant and an active listener is the ability to learn with and from each other. Concurrently with the point made above, the diversity of the meaningful texts is paramount to students being about to enhance their skills.

In relation to these skills, discussion pedagogy has shown to support student growth and development related to historical argumentation. Such a skill involves crafting an interpretive argument based on inexact evidence. In the case of historical argumentation and discussions, students will be able to "discuss evidence, plan for argumentative writing, and evaluate their peers' ideas" (Nokes & De La Paz, 2023, p. 333).

While the foundation of seminars and deliberations is cooperative in nature, it is clear that a bandying of conflicting ideas and thoughts related to the content or the situated problem will be presented in any type of meaningful discussions to which students are exposed. This begins with the fact that discussion pedagogy pushes students to develop an interpretive acumen that requires them to look beyond facts, dates, and events (Wineburg, 2001). For meaningful discourse to actually occur, students must think and process information differently than what would be required of them in teacher-centered approaches.

The ability to develop arguments and articulate their ideas is an important skill, not only for academic success, but also for success beyond the classroom. Students "must learn to read and write increasingly complex and specialized forms of text . . . [and] must go beyond telling what they know with the text, to engaging in knowledge construction, reasoning, and discourse with the text" (Monte-Sano & De La Paz, 2012, p. 275). When students are able to participate in such actions, it pushes them to analyze sources to construct historical knowledge and develop historical interpretations—based on both the text(s) and what is shared during the discussion itself.

Teachers have a steadfast belief that they want to push the envelope with students' thinking and the skills associated with that thought. This is such an important goal, but it is one that often goes unachieved. The problem begins with the fact that students often read texts and sources in a cursory manner. Moreover, they often read to be able to recite a *correct* answer—an answer that requires little to no interpretation. When the assessment is intended to produce such baseline responses, students pay little attention to what "the creator of the document [is] trying to say" (Schneider, 2014, p. 28). Thus, if you seek to help students develop their thinking skills, they must be provided meaningful opportunities that push them and that proverbial envelope.

Students, even the most skilled and accelerated, will likely need guidance related to executing a reading and situating their respective understanding to the central question shared with them. One way to scaffold support is by modeling four steps in the process. Students should be encouraged to (1) carefully read the document with the central question in mind, (2) paraphrase and annotate the document, (3) consider the perspective(s) of the author(s), and (4) write a summary or draft on how the text(s) relate to the central question (Dague, 2015). Such a streamlined approach will help students to develop their own understanding and argument related to the central question provided.

There might be some trepidation that students will not actually engage in the texts being utilized. This concern often stems from the fact that students are less than eager to read the prescribed pages from the course text. The fact is that most students do not actually read the textbook when asked. While we can push them to do so through reading journals or pop quizzes, this is still unlikely to get them motivated. The texts, as previously mentioned, need to be engaging while heightening students' interest. When students perceive the meaning as part of a larger discussion, it is likely that they will read with greater intent while potentially seeking out additional information to further craft their argument.

Students who were interviewed, as part of an action research study, talked about how the "dryness" of the book prevented them from wanting to complete the nightly readings. One student stated,

> I think the textbook readings, general speaking, are just dry. They're so dense; they have to fit so much information in. Seeing other readings like *King Leopold's Ghost* about Africa and Belgium [and] their conquest in Africa, the textbook glazes over that. That's not really talked about because it's so overshadowed by World War I and what else is going on in the world. (Dague, 2015)

The implementation of discussions pushes students beyond searching for what is considered *right* or *wrong*. As such, there is a more organic push toward analytical and synthetic thinking. This approach can present students with a unique opportunity to write with a greater purpose in mind. They will learn to understand that the need to develop opinions and those opinions must be based on their interpretation of the texts. While this might not happen right away, it is important to continue to work through the process *with* and *for* students. Students will develop and refine their thinking skills in order to understand the content while also being able to develop the arguments that will later be shared through the discussion itself.

FINAL THOUGHTS

The message is hopefully clear. Employing discussion-based approaches presents numerous potentials and possibilities. The other part of that message is that employing those same discussions can be a difficult and challenging as well as an iterative process. When you seek to push your students' thinking, and the skills related to that, you must begin first by meeting them where they are. In this sense, begin by taking small bites of that instructional apple.

For many students, being asked to probe, analyze, and examine texts for a later discussion can be frightening and, in some cases, off-putting. For some reason, after students enter into their middle school years, they are given so little time to delve into more thought-provoking topics. Perhaps this is a consequence of the system that has been created, pushing students to focus more on grades and being *right*. What is known is that the thinking and skills for which you are pushing are in each and every one of your students.

Keep a few things in mind. First, appropriate levels of scaffolding and patience will need to be on full display. This will support students in getting comfortable with the skills with which discussions will present them. Even in those moments where it might seem bleak to get any run out of the discussion, continue being reflective in all facets of the process. Give significant consideration to the texts being presented and what will pique student interest and drive them to push forward in the process.

Second, be mindful of where students are in that moment. For many, having such opportunities to be an active agent in this process can be new and unsettling. It is more than acceptable, and should really be expected, to share with students the rationale for the exercise with which they will engage. In many ways, they need to know that you are genuinely interested in their thoughts and that their voice does, in fact, matter. Providing them that reassurance might just be the first step to helping them move forward in the process.

Last, helping to progress students' thinking and the associative skills takes time. From argumentation and active listening to problem-solving and critical thinking, these skills will develop at different times and rates. Just like you need students being comfortable with being uncomfortable, you need to be the very same. Be prepared, flexible, and reflective. If you hold true to those tenets, discussions can create those authentic instructional moments where your students can grow now and for their future lives.

Chapter 10

The Change

One afternoon, one of my colleagues dropped by my classroom to say hello. More candidly, she also wanted to vent for a few minutes. Her expressed concerns revolved around the burnout she was feeling. She was an experienced teacher who was about seven years into her teaching career. She was an incredibly detail-oriented and laser-focused professional who really hit all the high notes when it came to the previously outlined characteristics of an effective teacher.

She knew her content, could manage her classroom, and was ultra-creative in her instructional planning and design. Perhaps most importantly, she loved and supported her students. Throughout our conversation, I just kept thinking that she just needed a new way to approach her classes that would challenge both her students and her. In essence, she had grown tired of using the same approaches she had been using in previous years.

I had just completed my doctoral work about a year earlier, and I was working on some new projects related to discussion- and inquiry-based approaches in high school social studies classes. In a leap of faith, I suggested that she and I work together to reimagine her instructional design and delivery. Admittedly, she was a far more creative and innovative teacher than I, and so I assumed I would get some type of collegial response that would suggest that we could think about such opportunities at a much later date.

Much to my surprise, she was on board and all in. In the coming weeks, we worked on identifying appropriate materials while also trying to discern the right moments to implement these new approaches. The delivery of the new materials, as we both expected, had a few kinks that needed to be refined. In time, and with a few modifications, her students began to really take to the new experiences they were having. This was not surprising given her acumen to develop thoughtful lessons. While her and her students' successes corroborated my previous beliefs regarding the efficacy of the instructional changes, it was not the most important thing that stood out to me.

What I saw was a spark in my colleague that was not there a month prior. Her excitement and enthusiasm was back, and every time she and I would talk, she had another new story to share about her students. In the numerous conversations that followed, she talked about her renewed passion and reinvigoration for teaching. The degree to which this occurred was truly unexpected. In one passing conversation, she mentioned how her new approaches created a change within her.

While we never took the opportunity to flesh out her ideas as to why, I believe that the change she was experiencing was a result of the fact that she, once again, began to believe in the power of her role as a teacher. While everyone around already viewed her as an effective educator, she began to feel those special things that come from the job we are, or will be, doing. This profession means something. Our role as agents of change should never go unnoticed or unappreciated.

The power to change the lives of young people is something for which we need to continue to strive. Through our creative and rigorous as well as relevant instructional practices, numerous possibilities exist for us to help develop lifelong learners. Embedded within those possibilities are opportunities to avail students as they learn to develop their voice through meaningful educational opportunities. In learning to use their voice and their burgeoning skills comes moments for them to grow in their understanding about the power they will one day hold as active participants in our democratic republic. While it can assuredly create a change for and in students, it very much has the same potential for us.

REIMAGINING OUR PURPOSE

In this last chapter, there is importance in reviewing what has been shared while also thinking through what it could all mean. In the forward path you seek to blaze in your classrooms and with your students, the first imperative is to begin with a clear vision. This vision should be one filled with positivity that can avail yourself and support your students as you chart your course and seek the actions you plan to take.

Ideas surrounding a change and reimagining your purpose are challenging to unpack in one chapter. Thus, an attempt will be made to do so through a quotation by noted American historian Charles A. Beard. Its use might serve as a conduit to clarify that vision and your reimagined purpose. While written nearly a century ago, the points he makes are still valuable and, in many ways, still hold true. Moreover, his words speak to the value and need for social studies teachers, and the field at large, to be recognized for the importance of the work attempting to be done.

In 1929, in an article titled "The Trend in Social Studies," he wrote,

> Amid all the fuss and feathers, there is substance, there is reality, in social studies . . . it will be said that the growth of social studies places on teachers an impossible burden, it compels them to deal with controversial questions. . . . They cannot master their subject reasonably well and settle back to a ripe old age early in life. The subject matter of their instruction is infinitely difficult and it is continually changing. If American democracy is to fulfill its high mission, those who train its youth must be among the wisest, most fearless, and most highly trained men and women this broad land can furnish. (p. 369)

Beard's position that the social studies has a unique substance and reality neatly aligns with the ideas shared early on in this writing. There has been tremendous fuss over the role and value of social studies education dating back to the early twentieth century. The history of social studies has been tumultuous, creating points of contention in everything from its definition to its status among other disciplines and fields. That tumult in many ways still exists today.

Buzzwords and sound bites exist today and focus on theories supposedly being taught and the potential indoctrination of students. This is, in many ways, where the misunderstanding about social studies education comes into play. Beard's points made about the substance and reality of social studies is one of the reasons that it will likely be in the crosshairs of public opinion forever. This will lead those in both public and academic ecosystems to opine over what should be taught and to whom. Given the fact that so much consideration is, and has been, given to social studies education, should tell us that there is a real value to the content being learned by students.

Further, social studies being so deeply focused on the study of man and society, there will always be changes and updates that will need to be made. This corroborates Beard's position that the subject matter is challenging because of how it is in a near-constant state of flux. What this means is that there will always be a need to stay abreast of the contemporary topics and issues—that which is associated with the content and society at large. More importantly, it also supposes the need to make sure that approaches being utilized are attuned to the needs of students. Our approaches must be thoughtful and creative as well as balanced.

When evaluating how to use discussion-based approaches, there must be intentionality in the materials presented and the questions being asked. In spite of our perception of the world and our ideological leanings, the task is to open up students' hearts and minds to all that exists. Discussions, whether they be seminars or deliberations, present those moments for students to recognize that which exists beyond the textbook and the proverbial four walls of the classroom. In sharing such balanced approaches and views, there is also a potential for our hearts and minds to be reopened as well.

As Beard also posits, an impossible burden is placed on teachers of social studies, meaning that teaching it, and all that it entails, is not for the faint of heart. As presented in the second chapter, there is a rhetoric that is strived for that is typically thwarted by the reality of various professional constraints. The questions and tasks that support the rhetoric of promoting students' civic-mindedness and democratic engagement are stymied by the actualization of high-stakes testing and state-driven curricular—both of which might appear inundating and antiquated. In our best attempts to work through potential impediments, there will be challenges.

What is important in these moments is the need to push forward and to persevere. In essence, motivated teachers produce motivated students. This field of study requires teachers who are willing to seek out and employ approaches that can support their students' needs. Authentic and genuine discussions are neatly situated to do just that. By providing students with instructional opportunities to delve more deeply into the content and the world in which they live, they will experience a place where their thoughts and voices can be both recognized and valued. Such moments are not something with which some students are accustomed. As such, the actions we take and the modeling techniques utilized will be important to the process.

Throughout the book, suggestions were provided for consideration regarding the design and delivery of both seminars and deliberations. Those suggestions were intended to support your efforts toward providing change while also supporting students' needs. The attempt to facilitate students' motivation, and more specifically their intrinsic motivation, is daunting. That being said, it is an aspect of the teaching and learning process that must always be considered in everything we do.

We must work to deliver on moments where students serve as co-investigators, explorers, and constructors of the content being learned. It positions them in unique ways to make decisions on how they want to go about working with materials and resources that do not end with formative and summative tasks requiring them to recite information in order to be *right*. This push to focus more on understanding—both of the material and each other—is far more valuable to them—in the moment and in their future lives.

Motivated students can become more self-actualizing in their worth and their abilities. As such, students who believe in themselves and actualize higher degrees of self-efficacy will be more likely to persevere through the challenges presented to them. The skills associated with self-regulation, both processes and actions, will stay with them as they embark on even more daunting and difficult challenges in their post-secondary lives. These are the skills that not only discussions can promote but that many authentic and engaging social studies methods can promote.

In evaluating the development of students' skills, discussions demonstrate unique correlations to the ways that students can learn to develop their abilities related to analysis, synthesis, and evaluation. While their progression up Bloom's Taxonomy might take time, discussions open opportunities for them to become deeply entrenched in rigorous and relevant materials that will be viewed as meaningful and worthy of their time. Additionally, their potential to develop and articulate streamlined and cogent arguments, related to questions being presented, will serve them well in both their academic and professional lives.

Discussions also present a unique opportunity to push students to move beyond communicating from behind a computer screen, mobile phone, or tablet. While the ubiquity of technology is here to stay, the soft skills that discussions can support will always be a necessity—irrespective of how technology evolves and impacts their daily operational spaces. Discussions can move students toward more robust critical thinking while also being mindful of the importance of serving both as active discussants and active listeners.

Behaving in both of these manners can lead to unforgettable moments where students can learn about the content while also learning about themselves and those around them. In forecasting its potentiality, students who learn to exhibit the skills associated with discussing and listening will be better positioned to operate effectively in our democracy. Candidly, this is where the change can begin for the health and well-being of our democratic republic.

As Beard stipulates, if our country will be able to fulfill what should be viewed as such an exceptional mission, then the skills required of it must begin right now. The skills and knowledge acquired in social studies classes throughout students' K-12 experiences can serve to defend and preserve this mission. The job that each and every one of us does to support such a mission should not ever be overlooked.

In conclusion, there is total agreement with Beard that trained professionals who lead our students undoubtedly serve as the conduit to the success of this nation. We should never allow ourselves to be viewed as just dutiful technicians and deliverers of information. We must never forget this as we begin thinking about the processes that go into our instructional design and delivery. This cannot be lost in the development and maintenance of the nurturing and safe relationships that all students need and want. This is not merely a job. This is a calling and a profession that deserves to be respected.

The hope is that this work, along with all of the great work that exists, pushes you to seek out new and genuine ways to work *for* and *with* your students. Your students and communities are depending on you. While the challenges will be imminent and the goal posts will periodically move, believe in your power. Seek out the challenge to push yourself and your students in ways that might have been unrecognizable. The time to reignite that passion for your students and the field is now. The time to support the principles and skills that have served as the bedrock of our democratic republic is now. Finally, the time to seek out and execute meaningful change must also begin now.

References

Alderman, M. K. (1999). *Motivation and achievement: Possibilities for teaching and learning*. Lawrence Erlbaum Associates, Publishers.

Angelo, T. A., & Cross, K. P. (1993). *Classroom assessment techniques: A handbook for college teachers* (2nd ed.). Jossey-Bass.

Apple, M. W. (2009). Controlling the work of teachers. In D. J. Flinders & S. J. Thornton (Eds.), *The curriculum studies reader* (pp. 199–213). Routledge.

Apple, M. W. (2018). *The struggle for democracy in education: Lesson from social realities*. Routledge.

Assor, A., Kaplan, H., & Roth, G. (2002). Choice is good, but relevance is excellent: Autonomy-enhancing and suppressing teaching behaviors predicting students' engagement in schoolwork. *British Journal of Educational Psychology, 27*, 261–278.

Ayers, W., Kumashiro, K., Meiners, E., Quinn, T., & Stovall, D. (2010). *Teaching toward democracy: Educators as agents of change*. Paradigm.

Bagenstos, N. T. (1977). *Social reconstruction: The controversy over textbooks of Harold Rugg*. American Educational Research Association. files.eric.ed.gov/fulltext/ED137190.pdf

Barth, J. L., & Shermis, S. S. (1970). Defining the social studies: An exploration of three traditions. *Social Education, 34*(8), 743–751.

Beal, C., & Bolick, C. M. (2013). *Teaching social studies in middle and secondary schools* (6th ed.). Pearson.

Bean, J. C., & Melzer, D. (2021). *Engaging ideas: The professor's guide to integrating writing, critical thinking, and active learning in the classroom* (3rd ed.). Jossey-Bass.

Beard, C. A. (1929). The trend in social studies. *The Historical Outlook, 20*(8), 369–371.

Benner, D. (2021, October 29). *Eight tips for practicing active listening in the classroom*. TCEA. https://blog.tcea.org/eight-tips-practicing-active-listening-classroom/

Blake, B., & Pope, T. (2008). Developmental psychology: Incorporating Piaget's and Vygotsky's theories in classrooms. *Journal of Cross-Disciplinary Perspectives in Education, 1*(1), 59–67.

Boesenberg, E., & Poland, K. S. (2001). Struggle at the frontier of curriculum: The Rugg textbook controversy in Binghamton, NY. *Theory and Research in Social Education, 29*(4), 640–671.

Bruning, R. H., Schraw, G. J., & Norby, M. M. (2011). *Cognitive psychology and instruction* (5th ed.). Person.

Carjuzaa, J., & Kellough, R. (2016). *Teaching in the middle and secondary schools* (11th ed.). Pearson.

College Board. (2013). AP European history curriculum framework, 2015–2016. College Entrance Exam Board.

Cormack, M. J. (1992). *Ideology*. University of Michigan Press.

Dague, C. T. (2015). *An action research study exploring the implementation of discussion pedagogy in support of student autonomy in advanced placement courses* [Doctoral dissertation, North Carolina State University]. North Carolina State University Repository.

Danao, M. (2023). *11 essential soft skills in 2023 (with examples)*. Forbes. https://www.forbes.com/advisor/business/soft-skills-examples/

Davis, H. A. (2003). Conceptualizing the role and influence of student-teacher relationships on children's social and cognitive development. *Educational Psychologist, 38*(4), 207–234.

Davis, H. A., & Dague, C. T. (2020). Teacher-student relationships. In J. Hattie & E. M. Anderman (Eds.), *Visible learning: Guide to student achievement* (pp. 153–159). Routledge.

deCharms, R. (1976). *Enhancing motivation: Change in the classroom*. Irvington Publishers, Inc.

Deci, E. L., & Ryan, R. M. (1982). Intrinsic motivation and teaching: Possibilities and obstacles in our colleges and universities. In J. Bess (Ed.), *New directions in teaching and learning* (pp. 27–36). Jossey-Bass.

Dewey, J. (2009). *Democracy and education: Complete and unabridged*. Feather Trail Press.

Eisner, E. W. (2001). What does it mean to say a school is doing well? *Phi Delta Kappa International, 82*(5), 367–372.

Eisner, E. W., & Cuban, L. (2013). *On teaching* [Commencement address]. School of Education, Stanford University. https://nepc.colorado.edu/blog/teaching-elliot-eisner

Engle, S. H. (2003). Decision making: The heart of social studies instruction. *The Social Studies, 94*(1), 7–10.

Ennis, R. H. (1987). Critical thinking and the curriculum. In M. Heiman & J. Slomianko (Eds.), *Thinking skills instruction: Concepts and techniques* (pp. 40–48). National Education Association.

Evans, R. W. (2001). *This happened in America: Harold Rugg and the censure of social studies*. Information Age Publishing.

Evans, R. W. (2004). *The social studies wars: What should we teach the children?* Teachers College Press.

Evans, R. W. (2006). The social studies wars, now and then. *Social Education, 70*(5), 317–321.Fenton, E., & Good, J. M. (1965). Project social studies: A progress report. *Social Education, 29*(4), 206–208.

Ferrari, B. (2012). *Power listening: Mastering the most critical business skill of all.* Penguin.

Fogarty, R. (1999). Architects of the intellect. *Educational Leadership, 57*(3), 76–78.

Freire, P. (2014). *Pedagogy of the oppressed: 30th anniversary edition.* Bloomsbury.

Glass, D. C., & Singer, J. E. (1972). *Urban stress: Experiments on noise and social stressors.* Academic Press.

Giroux, H. (1985). Teachers as transformatory intellectuals. *Social Education, 49*(15), 376–379.

Giroux, H. A. (1988). *Teachers as intellectuals: Toward a critical pedagogy of learning.* Bergin & Garvey.

Giroux, H. A. (2001). *Theory and resistance in education: Towards pedagogy for the oppression.* Bergin & Garvey.

Grant, S. G., Lee, J., & Swan, K. (2015, September). *The inquiry design model.* C3 Teachers. c3teachers.org/wp-content/uploads/2014/10/IDM_Assumptions_C3-Brief.pdf

Greenan, J. T. (1930). The case method in the teaching of problems of democracy. *American Journal of Education, 38*(3), 200–205.

Greene, T. (1954). The art of responsible conversation. *Journal of General Education, 8*, 34–50.

Grolnick, W. S., & Ryan, R. M. (1989). Parent styles associated with children's self-regulation and competence in school. *Journal of Educational Psychology, 81*(2), 143–154.

Harter, S. (1978). Pleasure derived from challenge and the effects of receiving grades on children's difficulty level choices. *Child Development, 49*(3), 788–799.

Harter, S. (1981b). A new self-report scale of intrinsic versus extrinsic orientation in the classroom: Motivational and informational components. *Developmental Psychology, 17*(3), 300–312.

Harter, S., & Connell, J. P. (1984). A comparison of children's achievement and related self-perceptions of competence, control, and motivational orientation. In J. G. Nicholls (Ed.), *Advances in motivation and achievement: The development of achievement motivation* (pp. 219–250). JAI Press.

Hertzberg, H. W. (1981). *Social studies reform 1880–1980.* SSEC Publications.

Hess, D. E. (2009). *Controversy in the classroom: The democratic power of discussion.* Routledge.

Hunt, L. E., & Metcalf, M. P. (1955). *Teaching high school social studies.* Harper & Row.

Huynh, T. (2017, April 14). *Three types of scaffolding: There's a scaffolding for that.* TanKHuynh. https://tankhuynh.com/scaffolding-instruction/

Johanningmeier, E. V. (2010). "A Nation at Risk" and "Sputnik": Compared and reconsidered. *American Educational History Journal, 37*(2), 347–365.

Jorgensen, C. G. (2014). Social studies curriculum migration: Confronting challenges in the 21st century. In E. W. Ross (Ed.), *The social studies curriculum: Purposes, problems, and possibilities* (pp. 3–24). State University of New York.

Jung, D. I., & Avolio, B. J. (1999). Effects of leadership style and followers' cultural orientation on performance in group and individual task conditions. *Academy of Management Journal, 42*(2), 208–218.

Keller, C. R. (1961). Needed: Revolution in the social studies. *Saturday Review, 44*, 60–62.

Kohlmeier, J. (2022). Socratic seminar: Learning with and from each other while interpreting complex text. In J. C. Lo (Ed.), *Making classroom discussions work: Methods for quality dialogue in the social studies* (pp. 63–72). Teachers College Press.

Kincheloe, J. (2008). *Critical pedagogy primer* (2nd ed.). Peter Land Publishing, Inc.

Kincheloe, J. L., & Steinberg, S. R. (1998). Students as researchers: Critical visions, emancipatory rights. In J. L. Kincheloe & S. R. Steinberg (Eds.), *Students as researchers: Creating classrooms that matter* (pp. 2–19). Routledge.

Korpershoek, H., Canrinus, E. T., Fokkens-Bruinsma, M., & de Boer, H. (2020). The relationships between school belonging and students' motivational, social-emotional, behavioural, and academic outcomes in secondary education: A meta-analytic review. *Research Papers in Education, 35*(6), 641–680.

Kumashiro, K. K. (2000). Toward a theory of anti-oppressive education. *American Educational Research Association, 70*(1), 25–53.

Lamb, A. (2023, March 13). *Do phones belong in school?* The Harvard Gazette. https://news.harvard.edu/gazette/story/2023/03/experts-see-pros-and-cons-to-allowing-cellphones-in-class/

Lee, J. K. (2005). Reconsidering the debate: Social studies, history, and academic disciplines. *International Journal of Social Education, 20*(1), 61–63.

Lepper, M. R., Corpus, J. H., & Iyengar, S. S. (2005). Intrinsic and extrinsic motivational orientations in the classroom: Age difference and academic correlates. *Journal of Educational Psychology, 97*(2), 184–196.

Lipstein, R. L., & Renninger, K. A. (2007). Interest for writing: How teachers can make a difference. *The English Journal, 96*(4), 79–85.

Logan, C. R., DiCintio, M. J., Cox, K. E., & Turner, J. C. (1995). *Teacher and student perceptions of classroom practice.* Paper presented at the annual meeting of the Northeastern Educational Research Association, Ellenville, NY.

Lyberger, M. (1983). Origins of the modern social studies: 1900–1916. *History of Education Quarterly, 23*(4), 455–468.

McKnight, D., & Chandler, P. (2009). Social studies and the social order: Telling stories of resistance. *Teacher Education Quarterly, 35*(2), 59–75.

McQuillan, P. J. (2005). Possibilities and pitfalls: A comparative analysis of student empowerment. *American Educational Research Journal, 42*(4), 639–670.

Monte-Sano, C., & De La Paz, S. (2012). Using writing tasks to elicit adolescents' historical reasoning. *Journal of Literacy Research, 44*(3), 273–299.

Nash, G., Crabtree, C., & Dunn, R. (2000). *History on trial: Culture wars and the teaching of the past.* Vintage Books.

National Archives. (2023, July 6). *What is the electoral college?* https://www.archives.gov/electoral-college/about#:~:text=The%20Electoral%20College%20consists%20of,of%20Representatives%20plus%20two%20Senators

National Council for the Social Studies. (2010). *National curriculum standards for social studies: A framework for teaching, learning, and assessment*. NCSS.

National Council for the Social Studies. (2013). *The college, career, and civic life (c3) framework for social studies state standards: Guidance for enhancing the rigor of k-12 civics, economics, geography, and history*. socialstudies.org/standards/c3

National Education Association. (2016, June 20). *By opening the door to cell phones, are schools also feeding an addiction?* https://www.nea.org/nea-today/all-news-articles/opening-door-cell-phones-are-schools-also-feeding-addiction

Nelson, M. R. (Ed.). (1994). *The social studies in secondary education: A reprint of the seminal 1916 report with annotations and commentaries*. ERIC Clearinghouse for Social Studies/Social Science.

Nelson, M. R. (1995, November/December). *The early years: 1921–1937*. Social Education. socialstudies.org/social-education/59/7

Niemec, C. P., & Ryan, R. M. (2009). Autonomy, competence, and relatedness in the classroom. *Theory and Research in Education, 7*(2), 133–144.

Noddings, N. (1988). An ethic of caring and its implications for instructional arrangements. *American Journal of Education, 96*(2), 215–230.

Nokes, J. D., & De La Paz, S. (2023). Historical argumentation: Watching historians and teaching youth. *Written Communication, 40*(2), 333–372.

Parker, W. C. (1996). "Advanced" ideas about democracy: Toward a pluralist conception of citizen education. *Teachers Record College, 98*(1), 105–125.

Parker, W. C. (1997). The art of deliberation. *Educational Leadership, 54*(5), 18–21.

Parker, W. C. (2001). Educating democratic citizens: A broad view. *Theory into Practice, 40*(1), 6–13.

Parker, W. C. (2003). *Teaching democracy: Unity and diversity in public life*. Teachers College Press.

Parker, W. C. (2004). Knowing and doing in democratic citizenship education. In L. S. Levstik & C. A. Tyson (Eds.), *Handbook of research in social studies education* (pp. 65–80). Routledge.

Parker, W. C. (2006). Public discourses in schools: Purposes, problems, possibilities. *Educational Researcher, 35*(8), 11–18.

Parker, W. (2010). Listening to strangers: Classroom discussion in democratic education. *Teachers Record College, 112*(11), 2815–2832.

Parker, W. C., & Hess, D. (2001). Teacher with and for discussion. *Teaching and Teacher Education, 17*, 273–289.

PBS Newshour. (2022, November 4). *Parents pushback on cellphones bans at school*. https://www.pbs.org/newshour/education/parents-pushback-on-cellphone-bans-at-school#:~:text=As%20growing%20numbers%20of%20schools,before%20the%20COVID%2D19%20pandemic

Pelletier, L. G., & Rocchi, M. (2016). Teachers' motivation in the classroom. In L. W. Chia, J. W. C. Keng, & R. Ryan (Eds.), *Building autonomous learners:*

Perspectives from research and practice using self-determination theory (pp. 107–128). Springer.

Phillips, J. (1996). *Society, state, and nation in twentieth-century Europe.* Prentice-Hall.

Radvansky, G. A., & Ashcraft, M. H. (2018). *Cognition* (7th ed.). Pearson.

Ravitch, D. R., & Finn, Jr., C. E. (1987). *What do our 17-year-olds know? A report on the first national assessment of history and literature.* Harper & Row.

Reeve, J. (2006). Teachers as facilitators: What autonomy-supportive teachers do and why their students benefit. *The Elementary School Journal, 106*(3), 225–236.

Reeve, J. (2009). Why teachers adopt a controlling motivating style toward students and how they can become more autonomy supportive. *Educational Psychologist, 44*(3), 159–175.

Reeve, J. (2016). Autonomy-supportive teaching: What it is, how to do it. In L. W. Chia, J. W. C. Keng, & R. Ryan (Eds.), *Building autonomous learners: Perspectives from research and practice using self-determination theory* (pp. 129–152). Springer.

Reeve, J., & Halusic, M. (2009). How K-12 teachers can put self-determination theory principles into practice. *Theory and Research in Education, 7*(2), 145–154.

Ryan, R. M., & Deci, E. L. (2000). Self-determination theory and the facilitation of intrinsic motivation, social development, and well-being. *American Psychologist, 55*(1), 68–78.

Ryan, R. M., & Deci, E. L. (2018). *Self-determination theory: Basic psychological needs in motivation, development, and wellness.* The Guilford Press.

Santrock, J. W. (2020). *Educational psychology* (7th ed.). McGraw-Hill.

Saxton, J., Miller, C., Laidlaw, L., & O'Mara, J. (2018). *Asking better questions: Teaching and learning for a changing world* (3rd ed.). Pembroke Publishers.

Schneider, D. (2014). Exploring disciplinary literacy: Academic writing in history classes. *Social Studies Review, 53,* 28–36.

Schunk, D. H., Pintrich, P. R., & Meece, J. L. (2008). *Motivation in education: Theory, research, and applications* (3rd ed.). Pearson Education, Inc.Selsky, A. (2020, December 2020). *How do other democratic nations select leaders?* The Associated Press. https://kslnewsradio.com/1938616/explainer-how-do-other-democratic-nations-select-leaders/

Spataro, S. E., & Block, J. (2018). "Can you repeat that?" Teaching active listening in management education. *Journal of Management Education, 42*(2), 168–198.

Stanley, W. B. (2005). Social studies and the social order: Transmission or transformation? *Social Education, 69*(5), 282–287.

Stearns, P. N. (1998). *Why study history?* American Historical Association. https://www.historians.org/about-aha-and-membership/aha-history-and-archives/historical-archives/why-study-history-(1998)

Stefanou, C. R., Perencevich, K. C., DiCinto, M., & Turner, J. C. (2004). Supporting autonomy in the classroom: Ways teachers encourage student decision making and ownership. *Educational Psychology, 39,* 97–110.

Swan, K. (2013). The importance of the c3 framework. *Social Education, 77*(4), 222–224.

Swan, K., Lee, J., & Grant, S. G. (2018). *Inquiry design model: Building inquiries in social studies*. National Council for the Social Studies and C3 Teaches.

The Heritage Foundation. (2023). *The benefits*. https://www.heritage.org/the-essential-electoral-college/the-benefits

The National Commission on Excellence in Education. (1983). *A nation at risk: The imperative for educational reform*. edreform.com/wp-content/uploads/2013/01/A_Nation_At_Risk_1983.pdf

Weger, H., Castle, G. R., & Emmett, M. C. (2010). Active listening in peer interviews: The influence of message paraphrasing on perceptions on listening skill. *International Journal of Listening, 24*, 34–49.

West, D. M. (2019, October 15). *It's time to abolish the electoral college system*. Brookings. https://www.brookings.edu/articles/its-time-to-abolish-the-electoral-college/

White, S. K. (1991). *Political theory and postmodernism*. Cambridge University Press.

Wineburg, S. (2001). *Historical thinking and other unnatural acts: Charting the future of teaching the past*. Temple University Press.

Wineburg, S. (2018). *Why learn history (when it's already on your phone)*. The University of Chicago Press.

Zinn, H. (1999). *A people's history of the United States*. Harper Perennial.

About the Author

A former high school social studies teacher and head baseball coach, **Dr. Christopher Dague** has melded his past experience in education and motivational theory with his present expertise in curriculum and instruction. The author of numerous peer-reviewed articles and invited essays in the field, he currently serves as an associate professor of teacher and social studies education at The Citadel in Charleston, South Carolina.